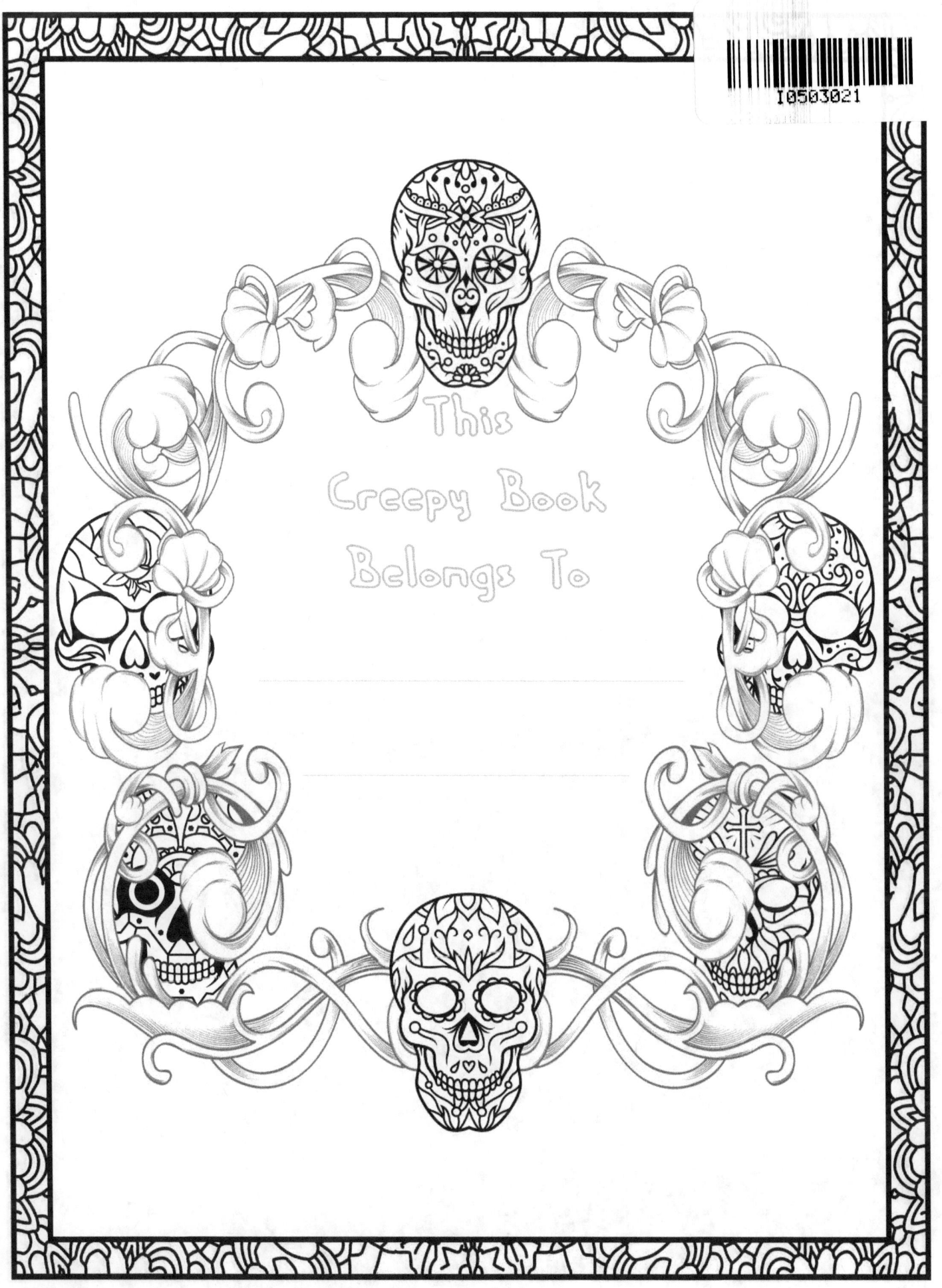

This

Creepy Book

Belongs To

Test Your Colors on this page to see how they react to the paper.
Place a blank piece of paper (or two) behind each coloring page as you color, to prevent bleed-through to the next page.

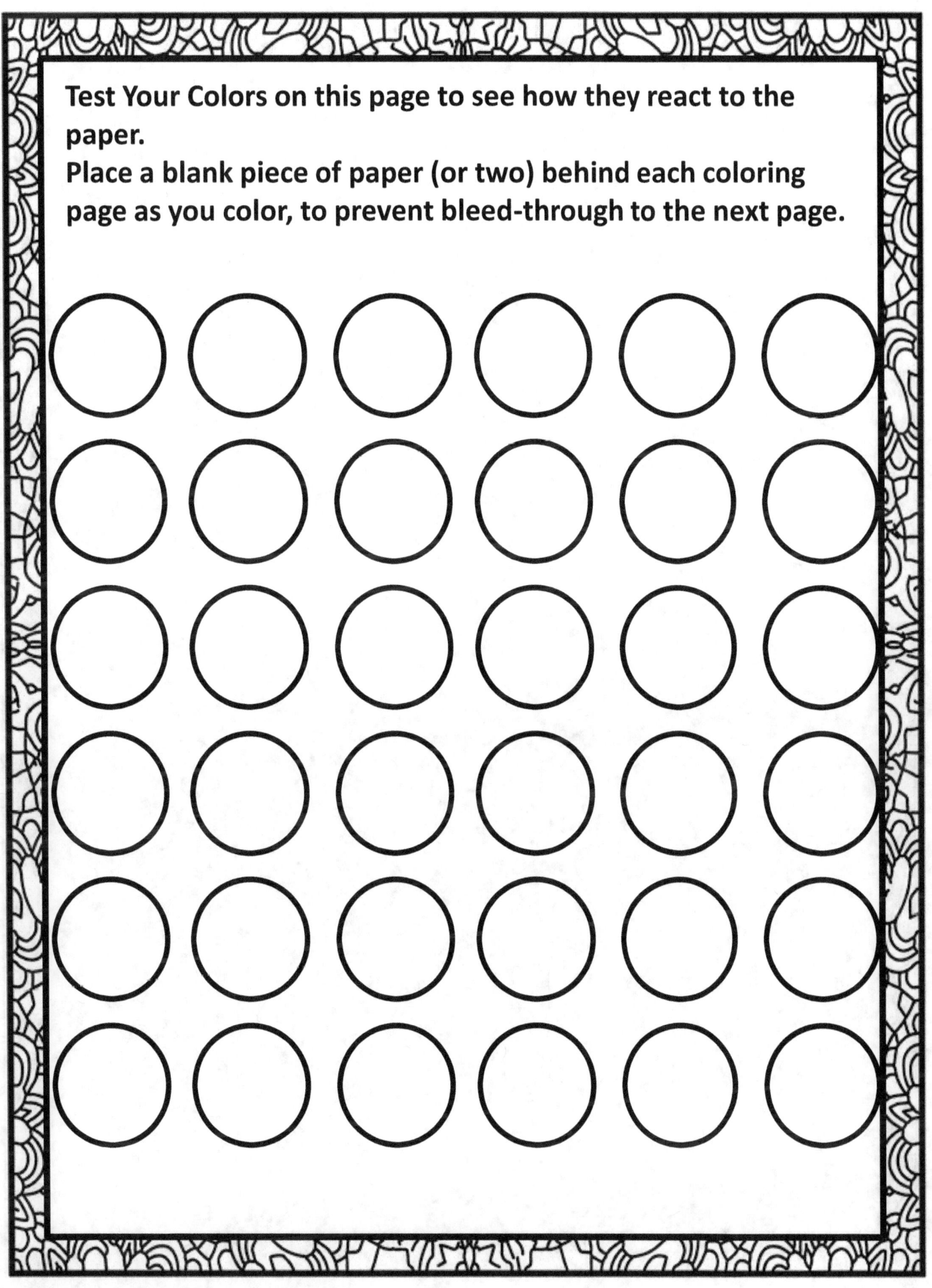

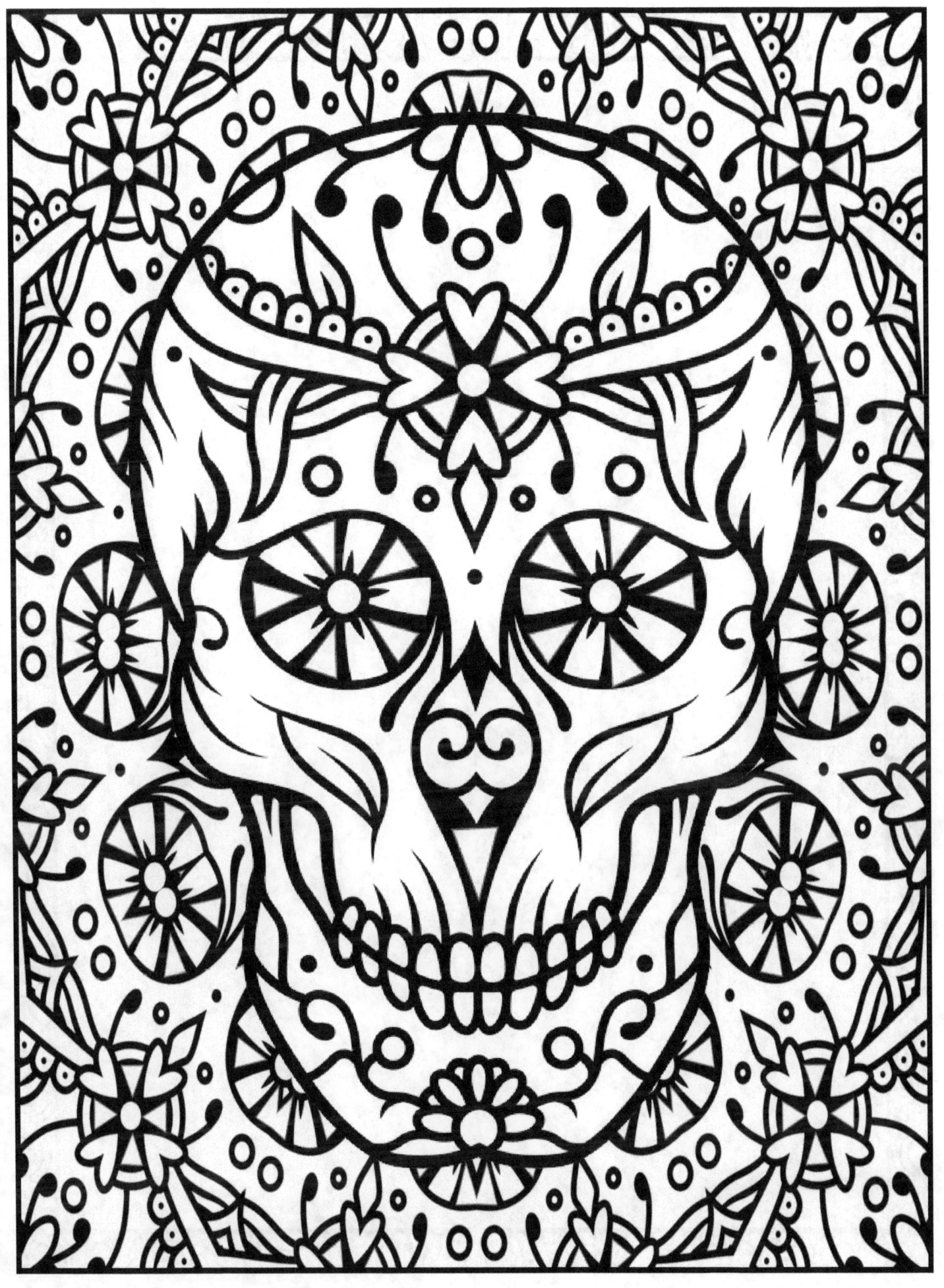

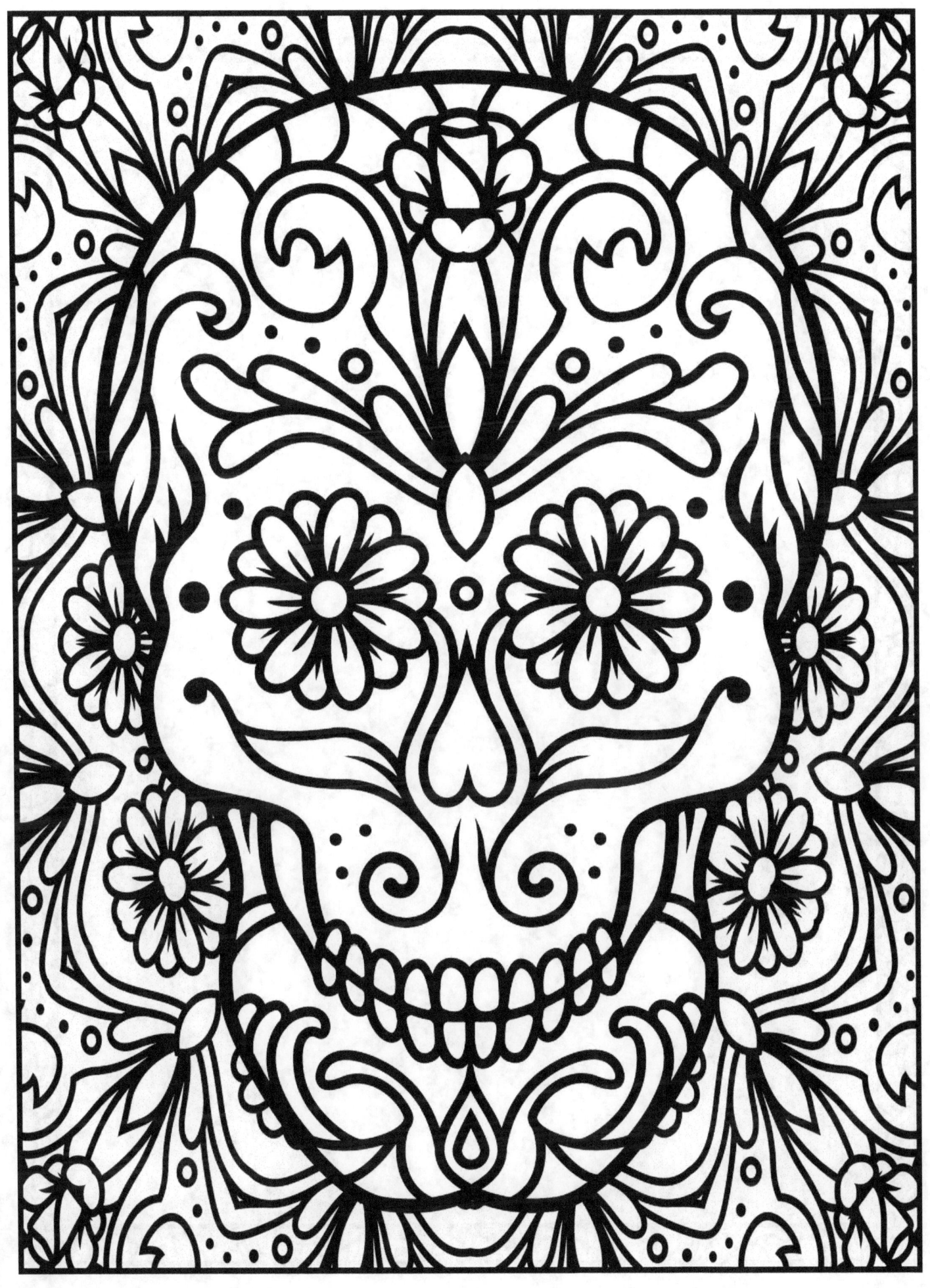

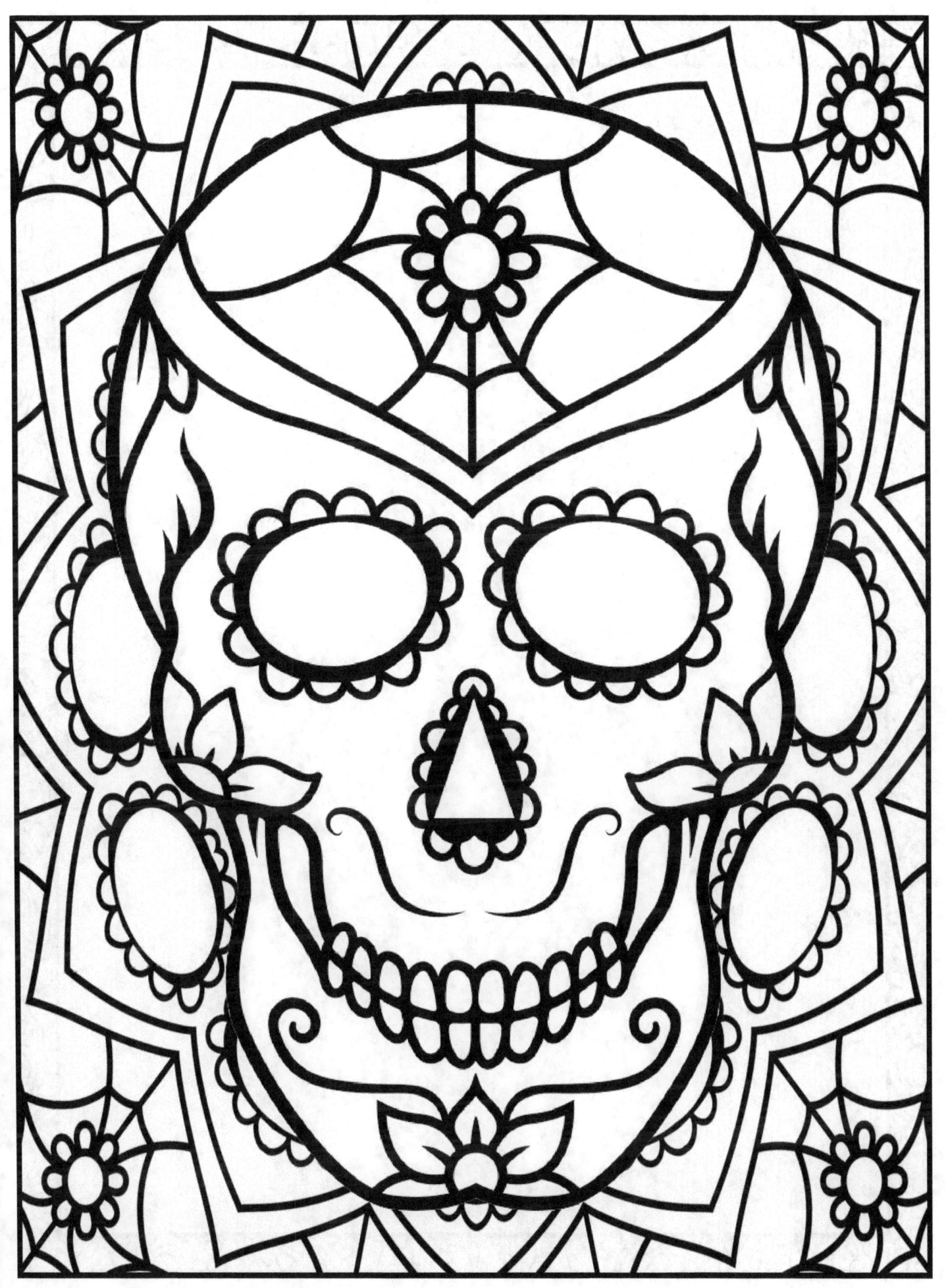

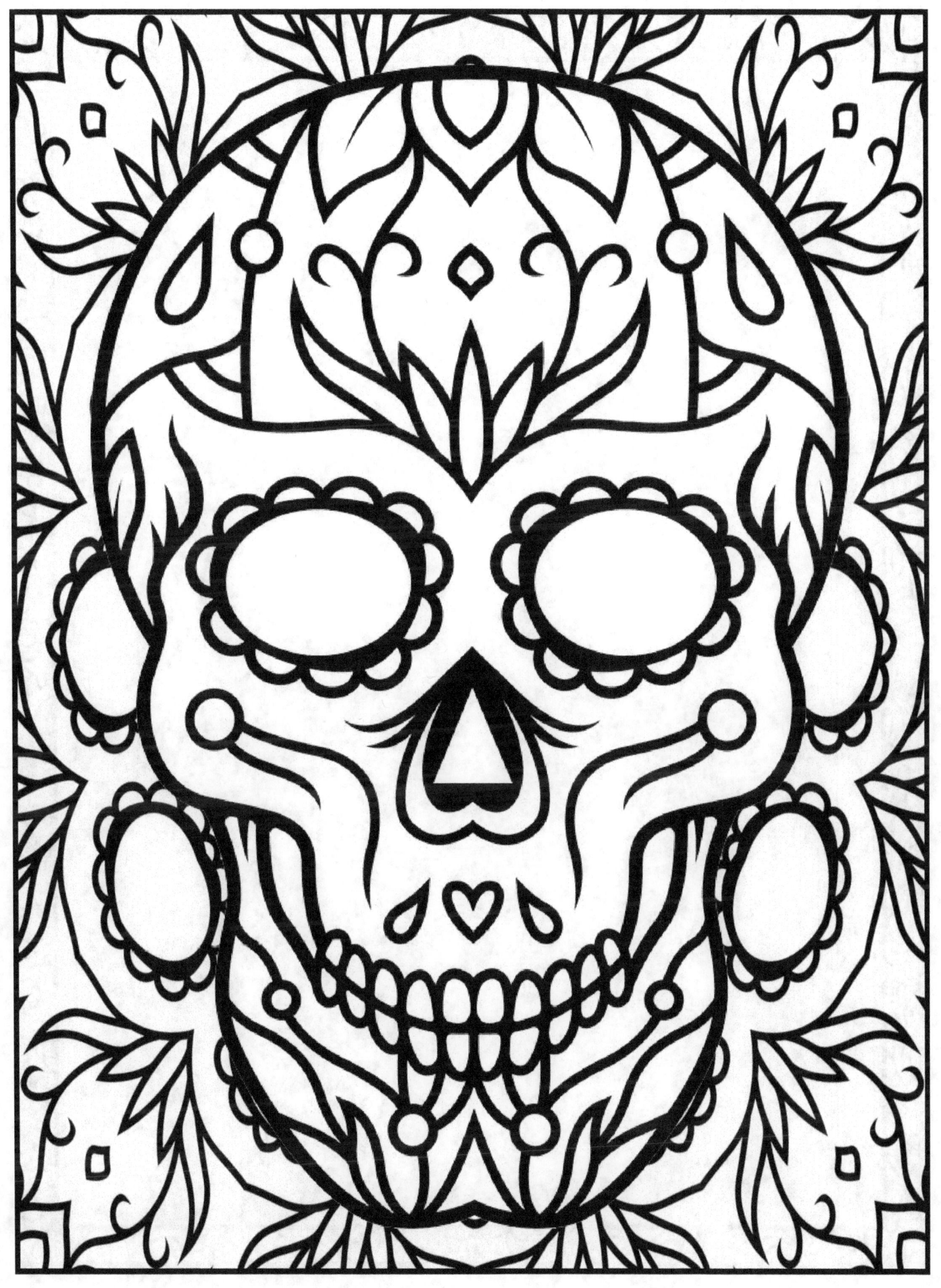

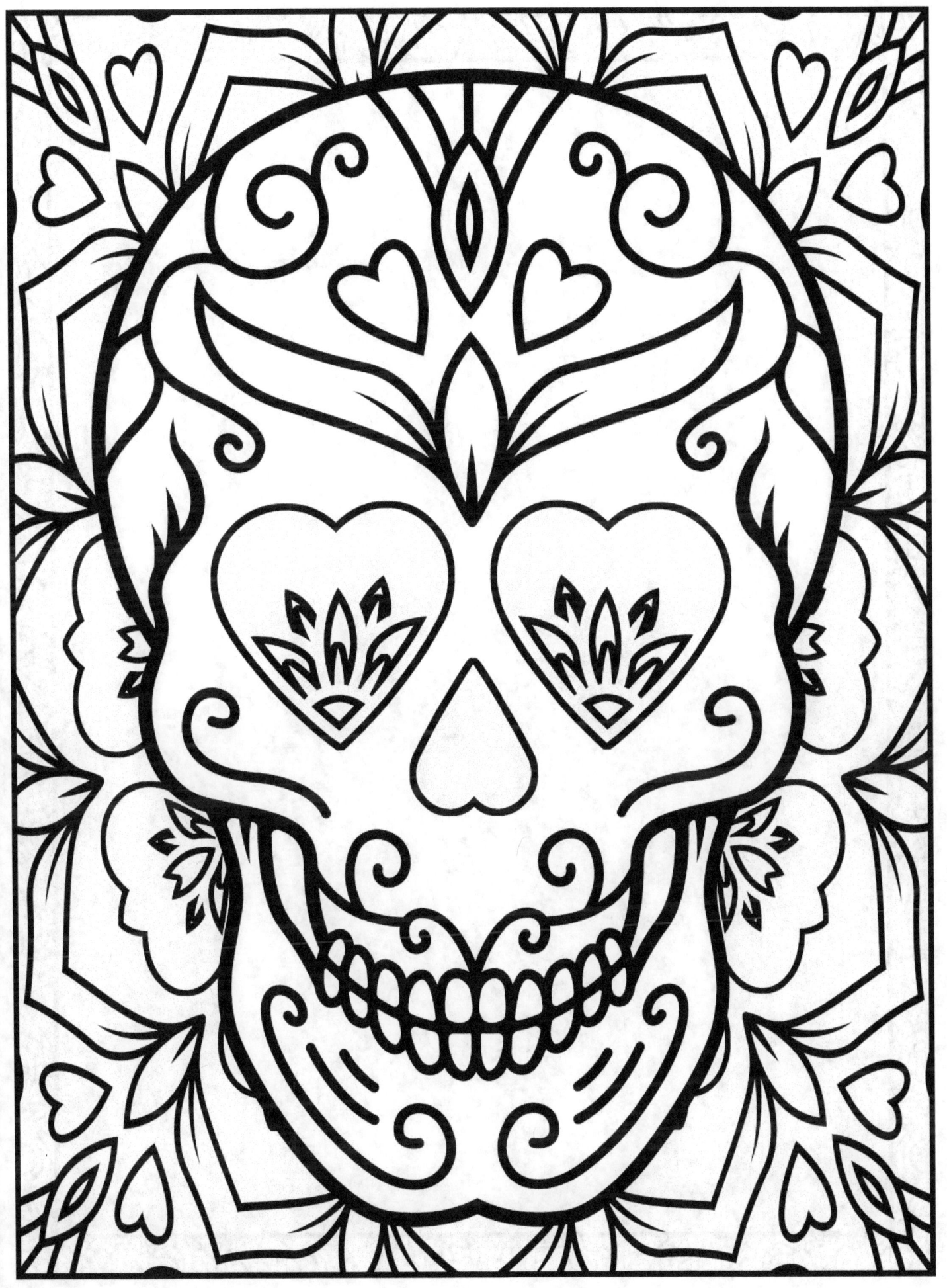

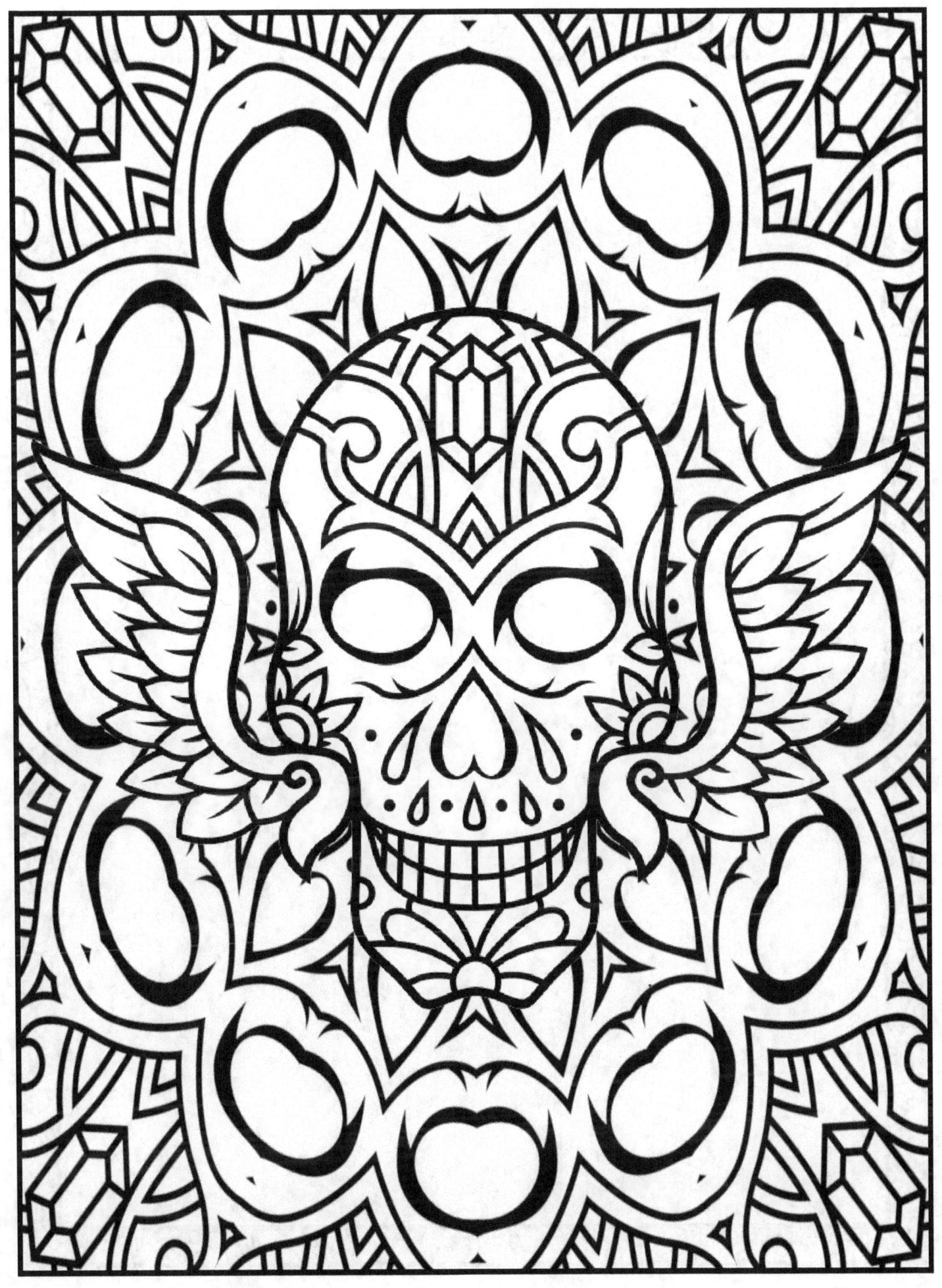

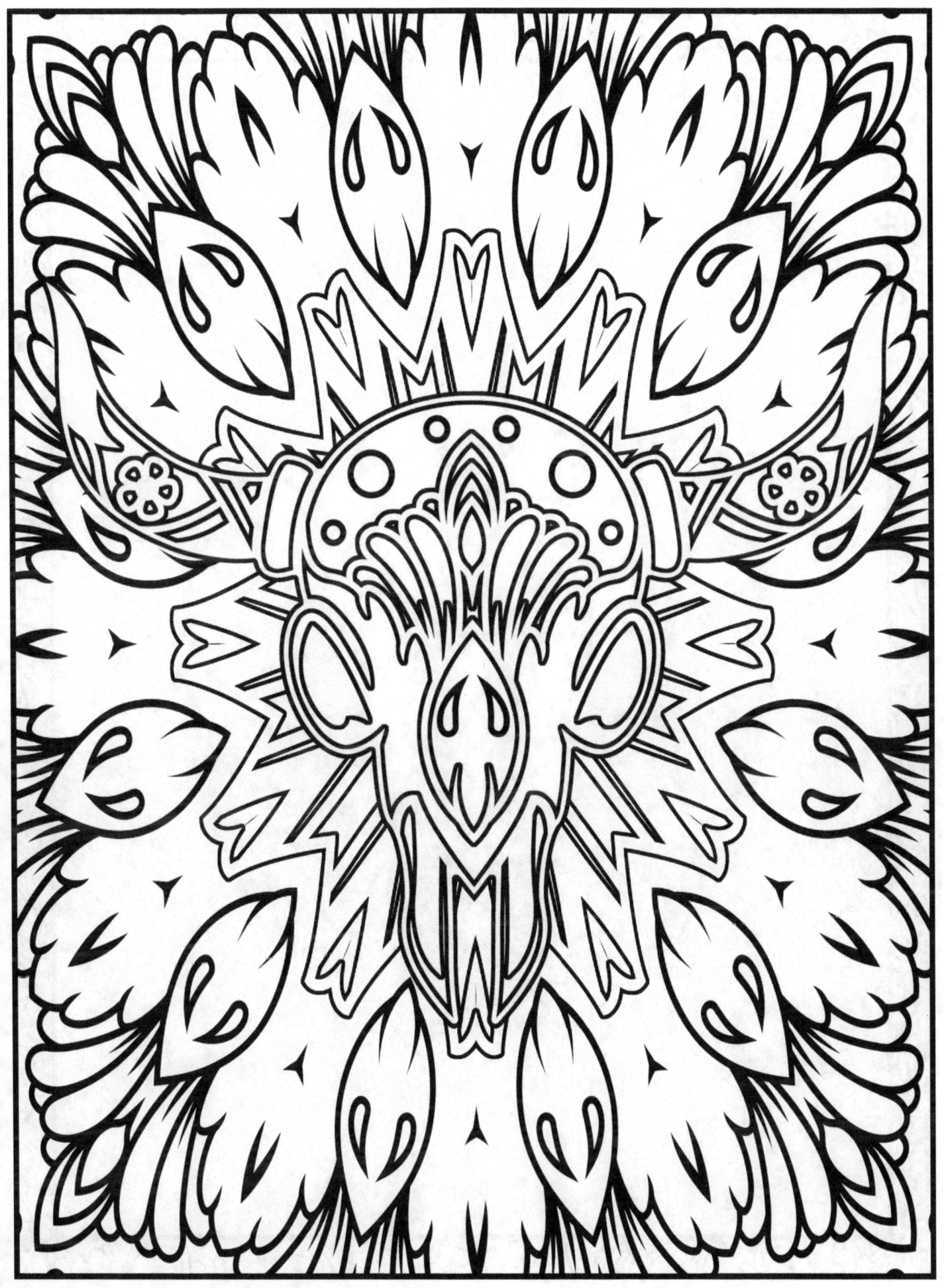

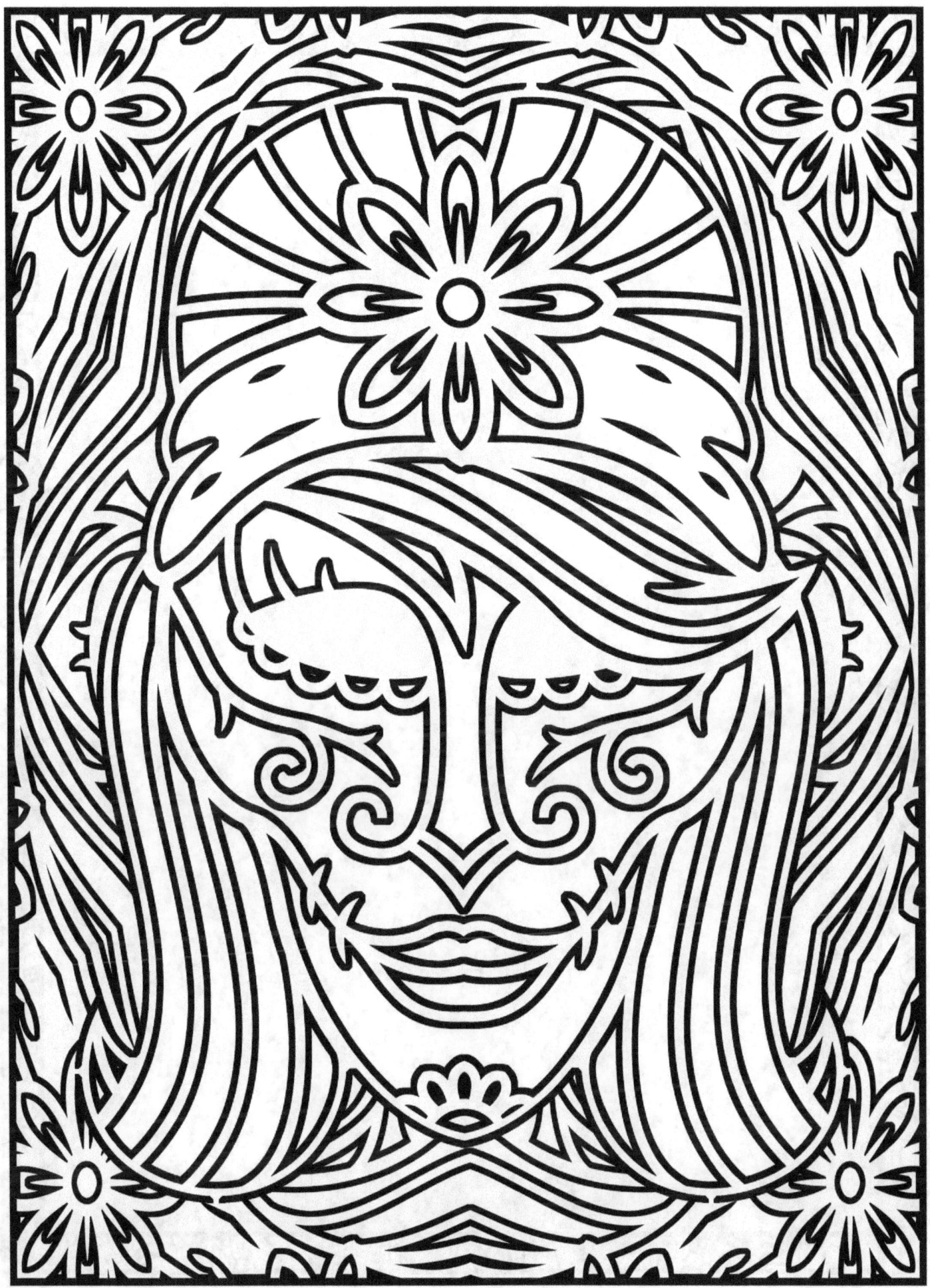

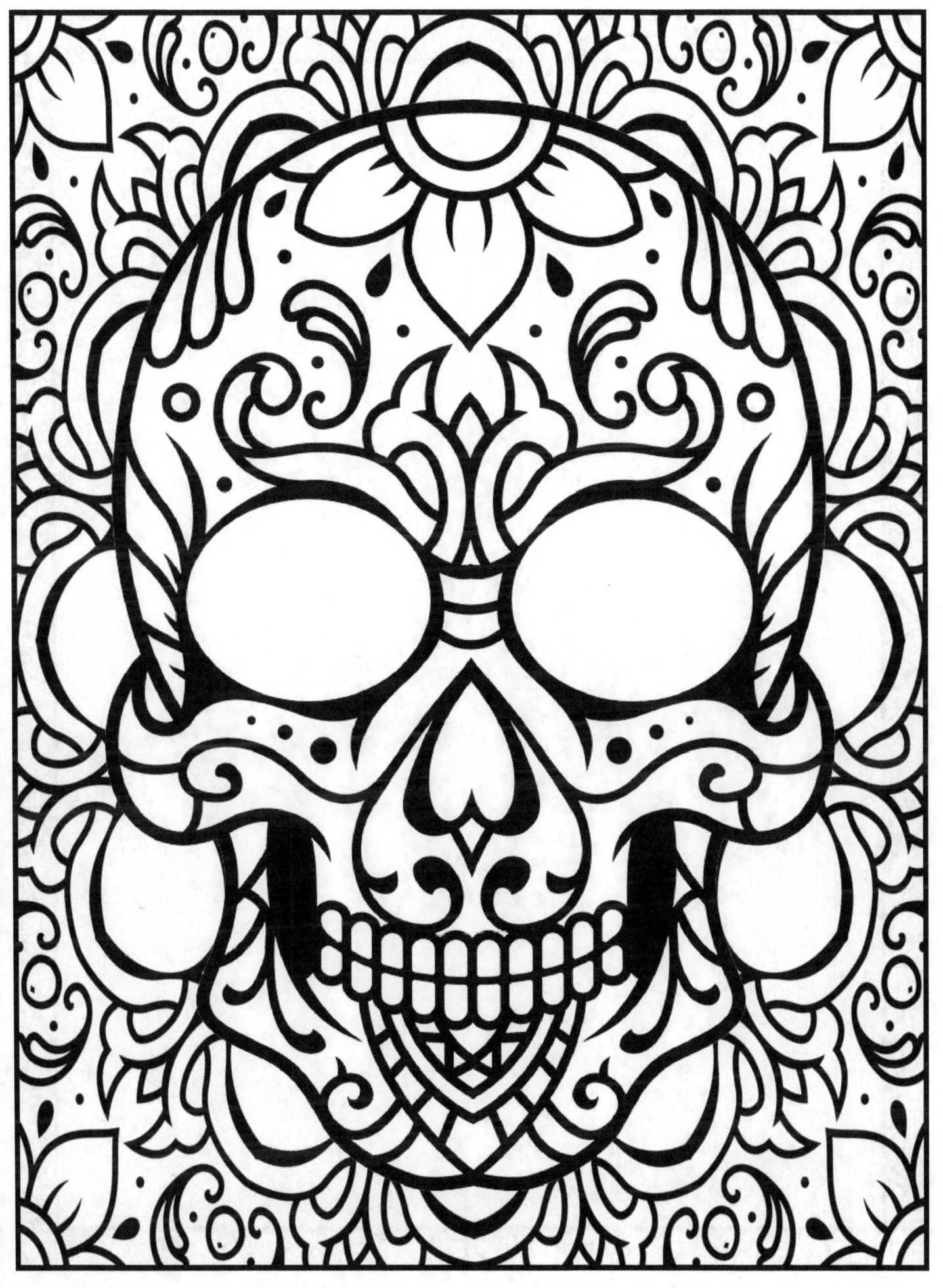

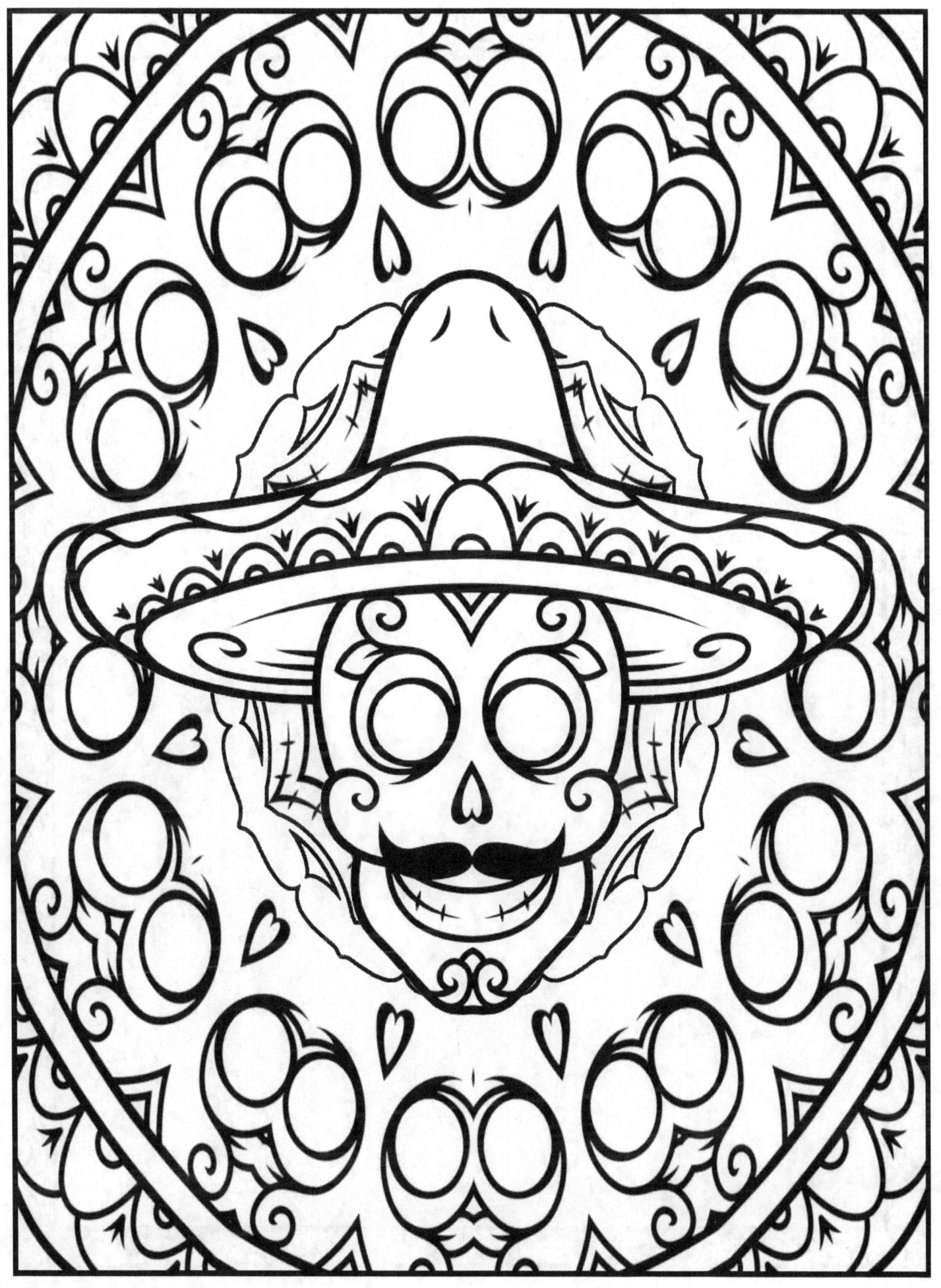

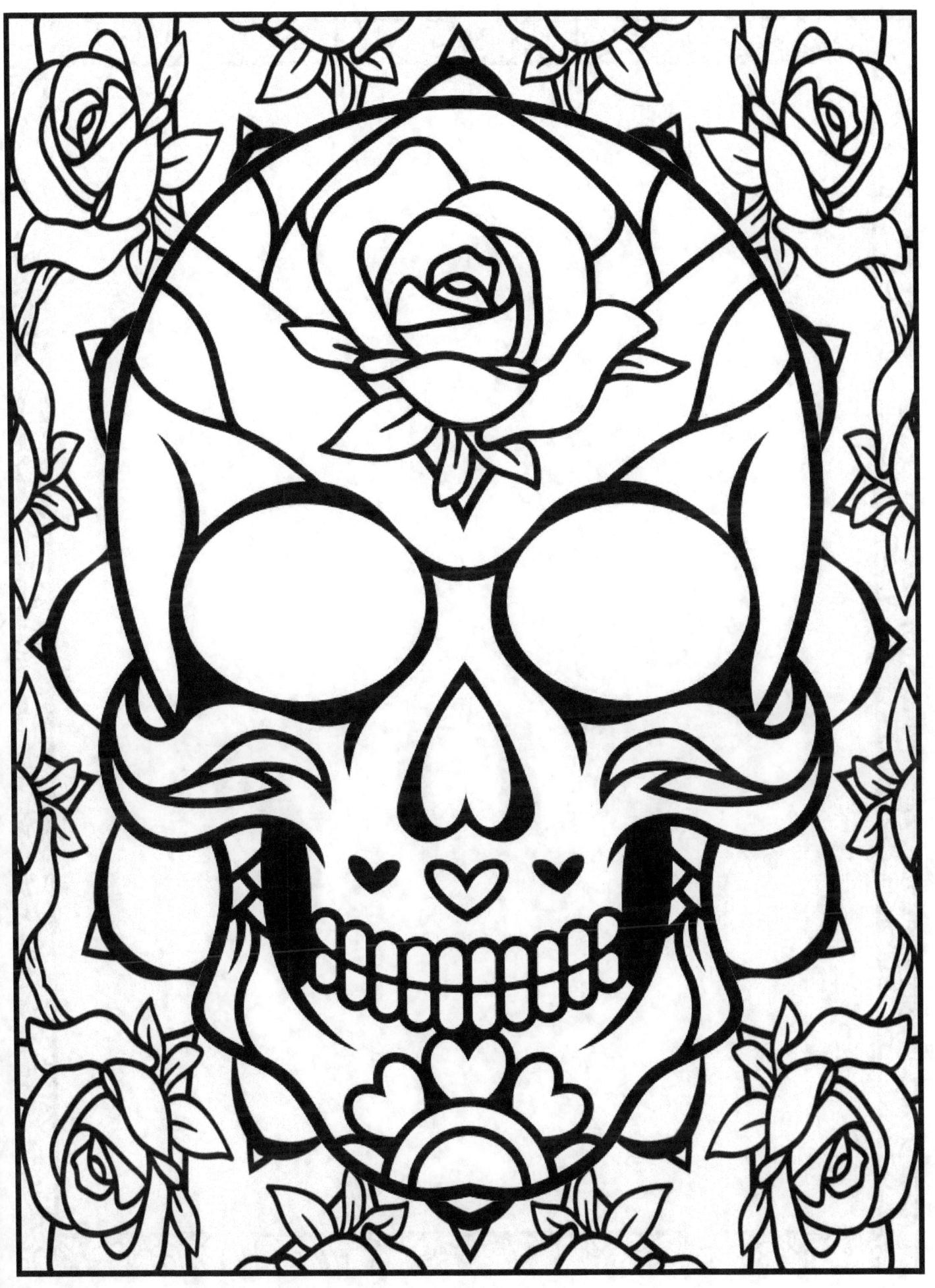

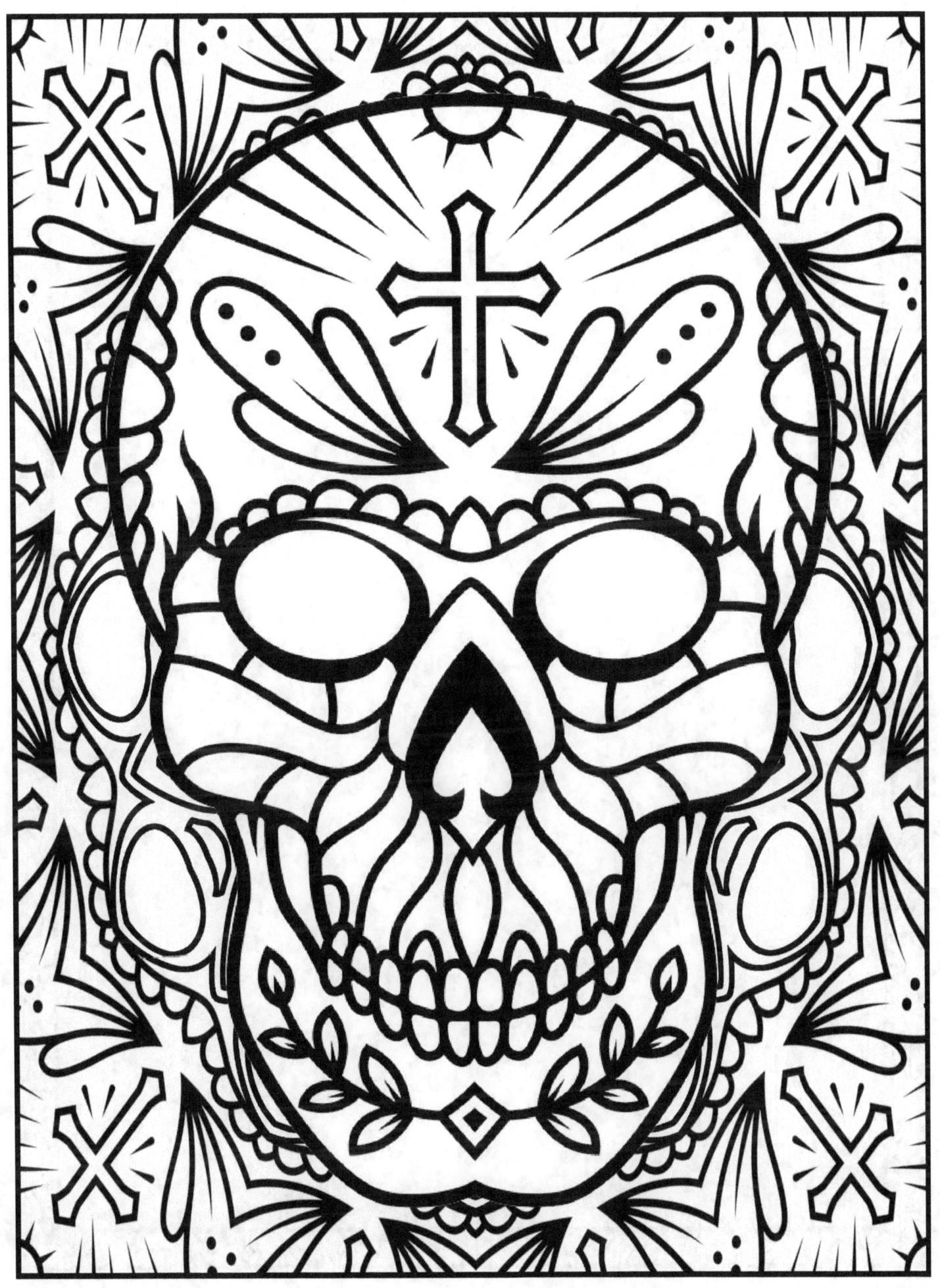

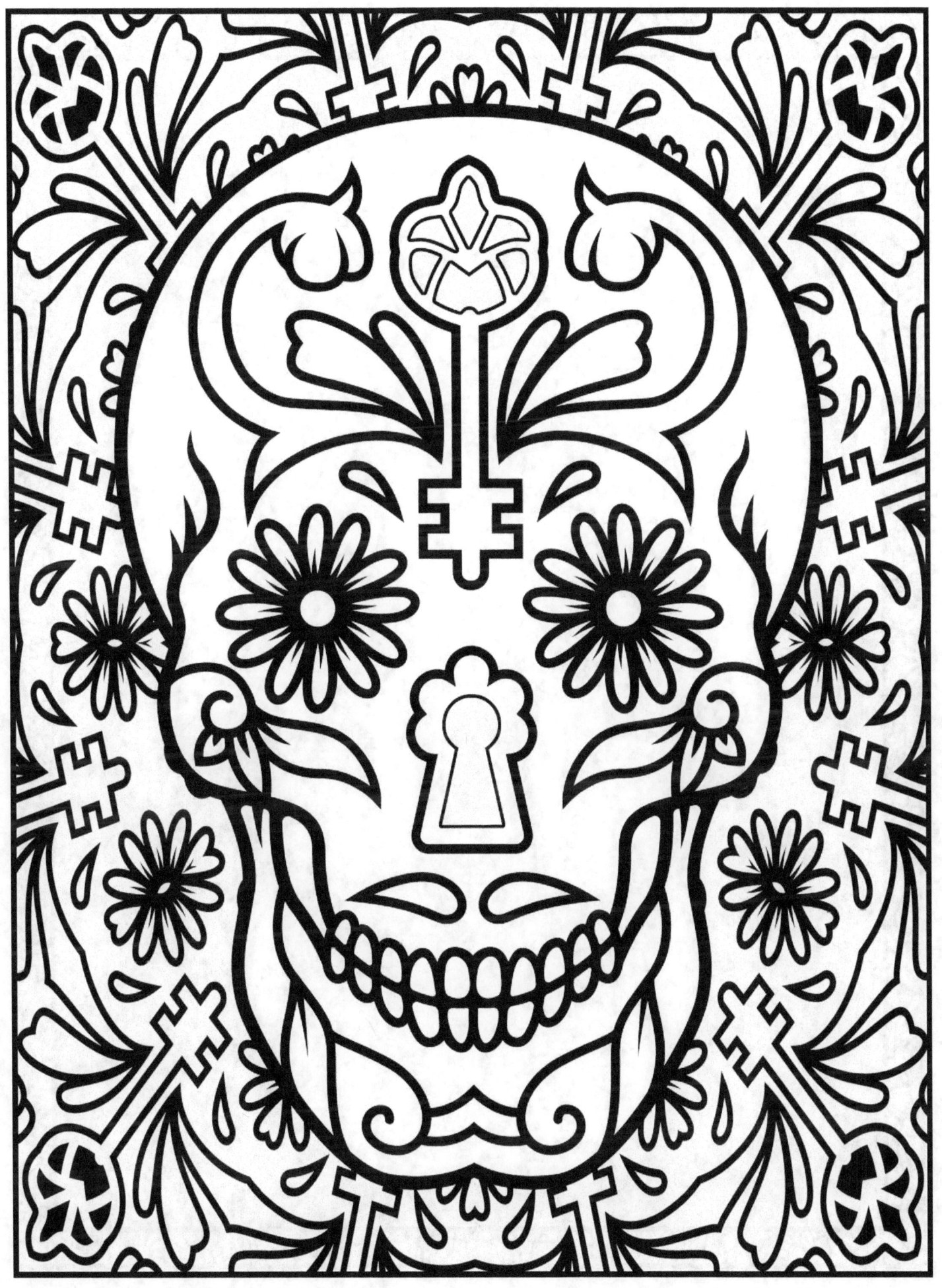

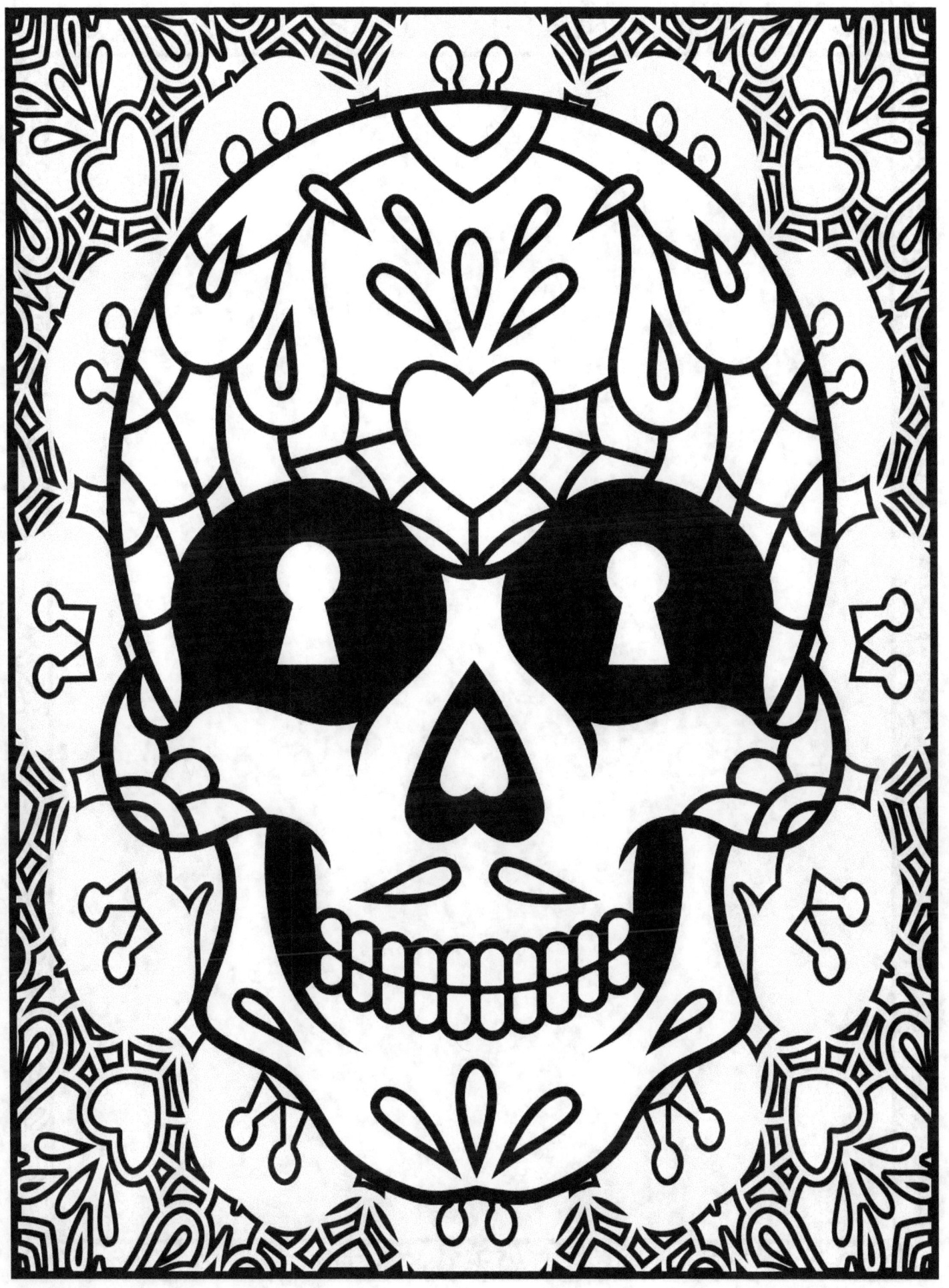

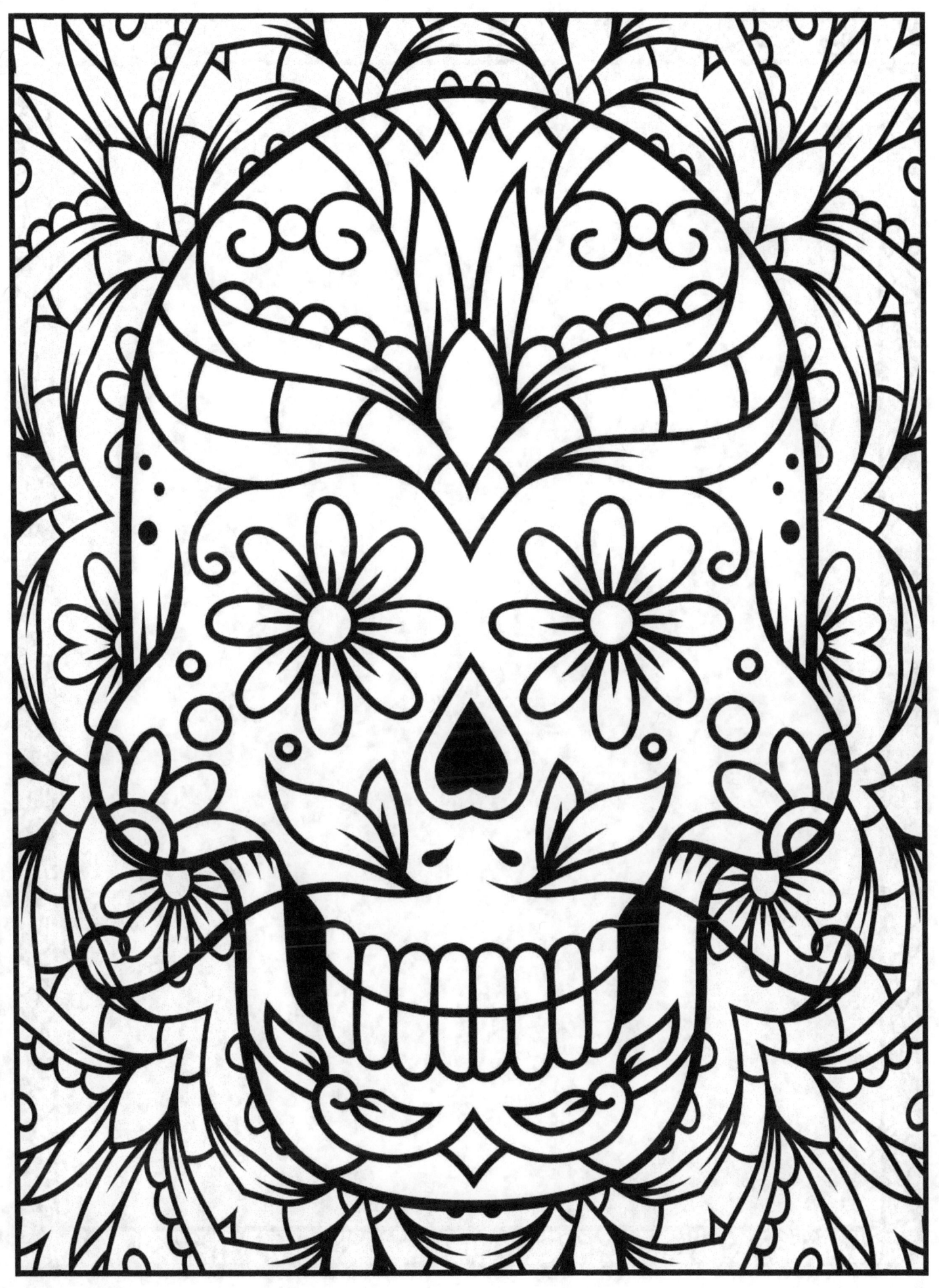

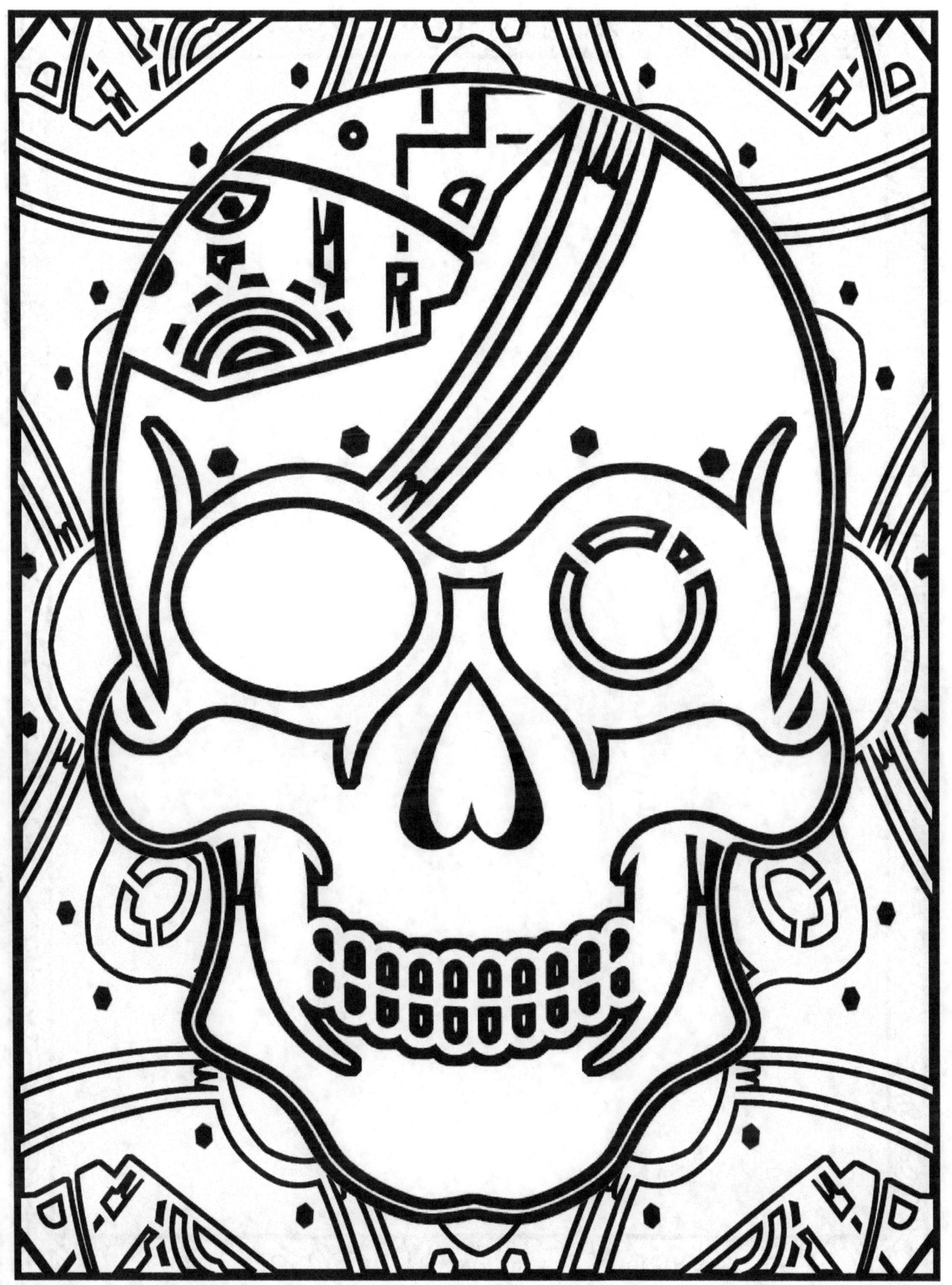

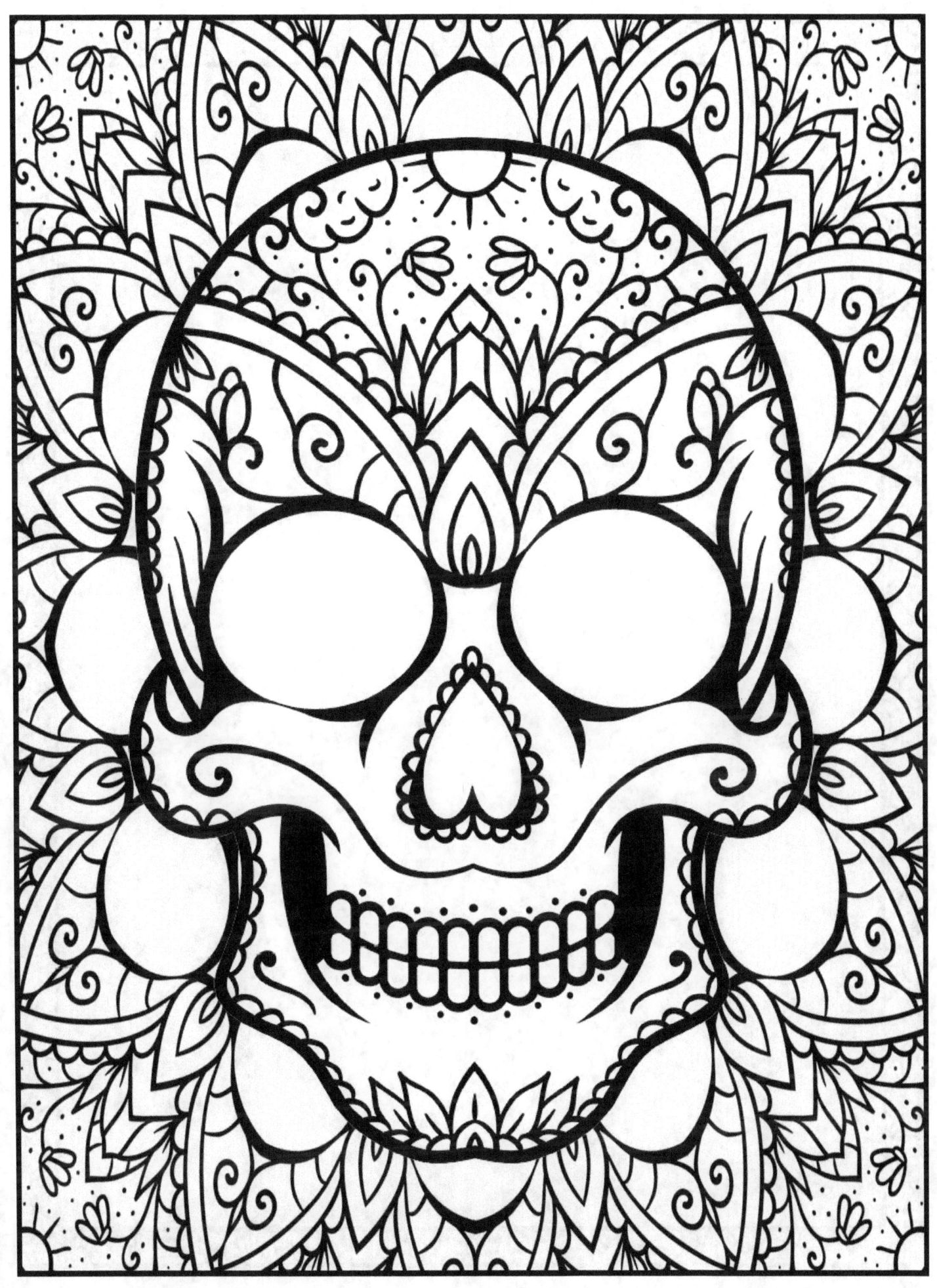

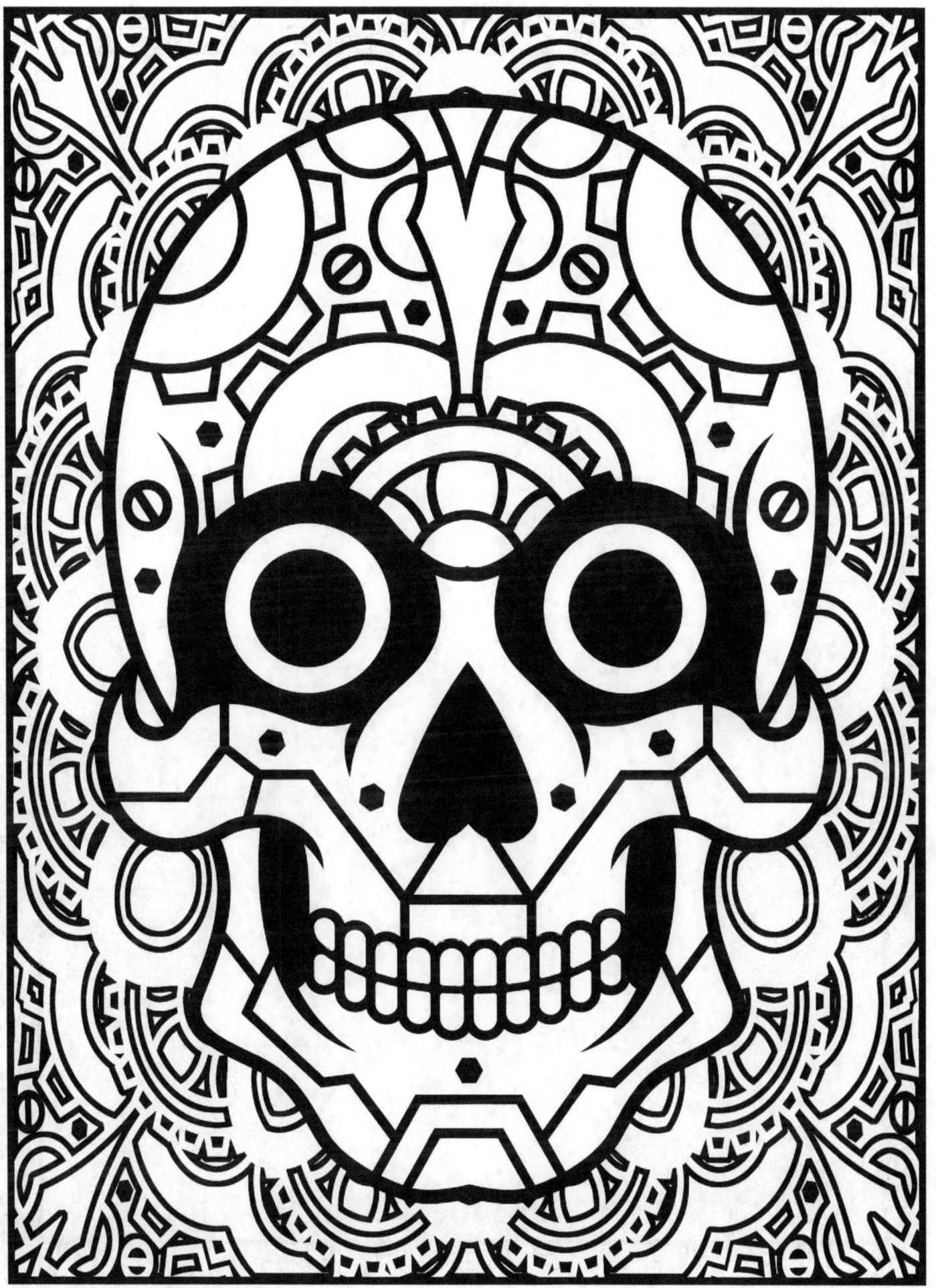

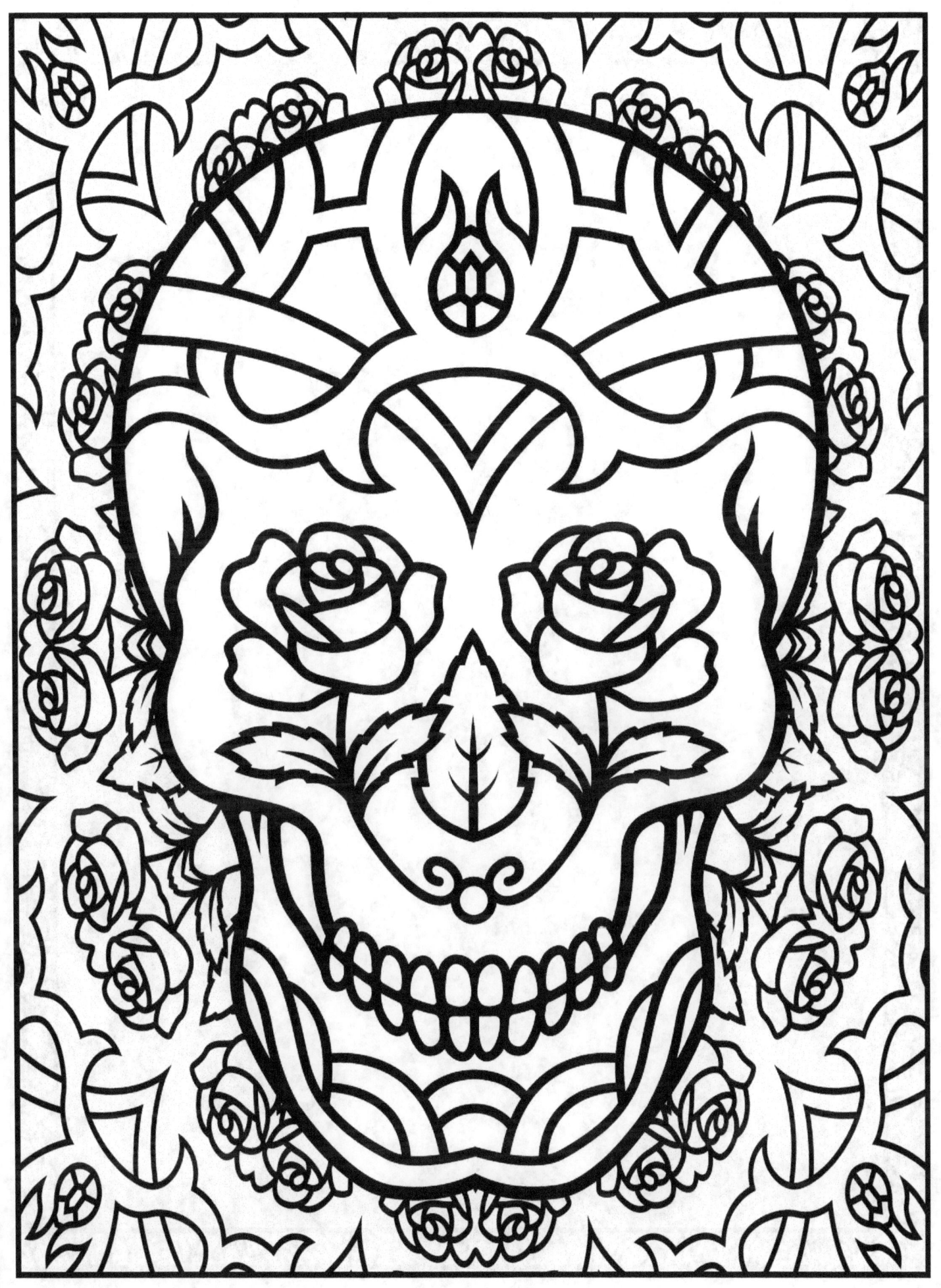

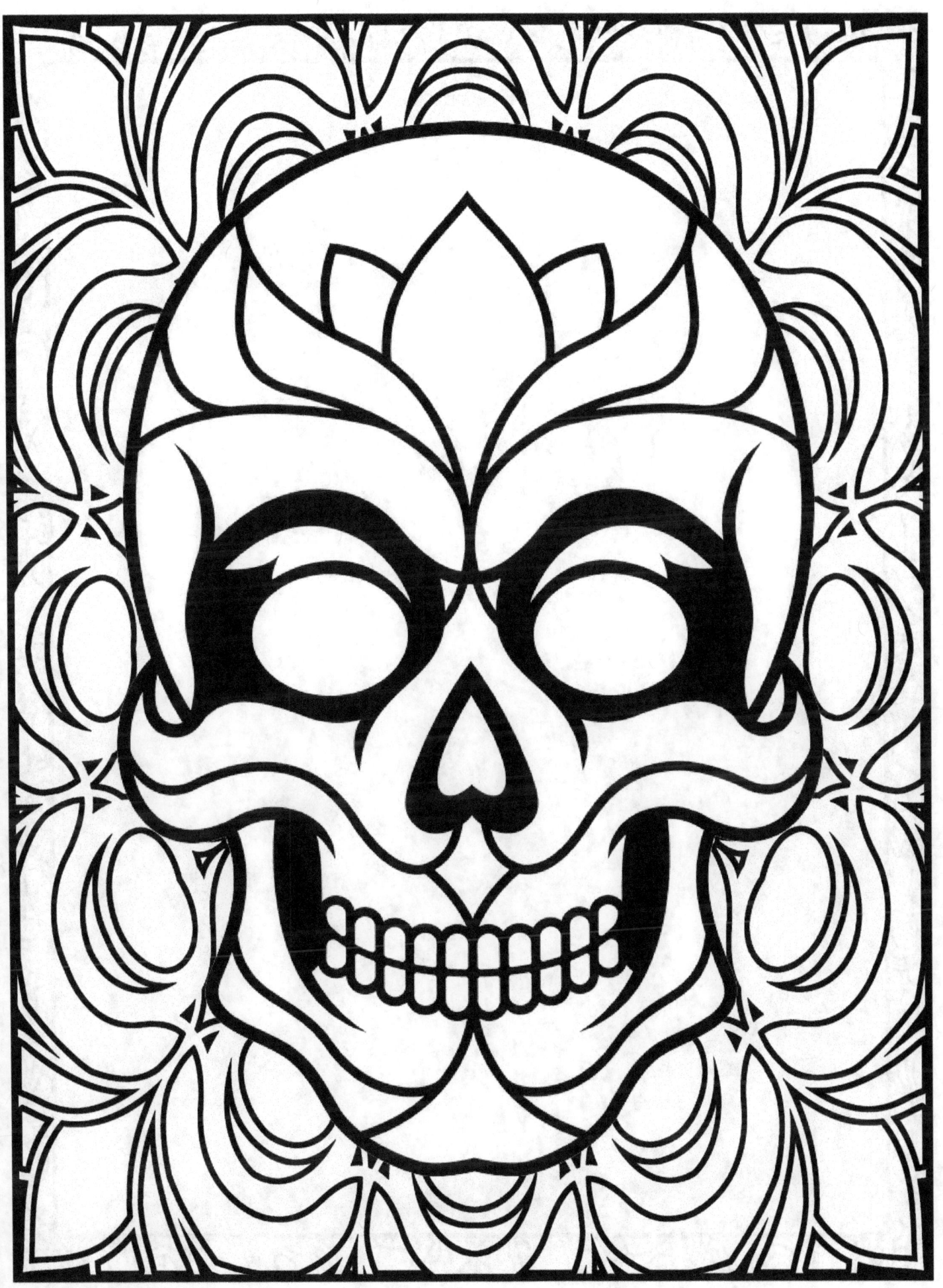

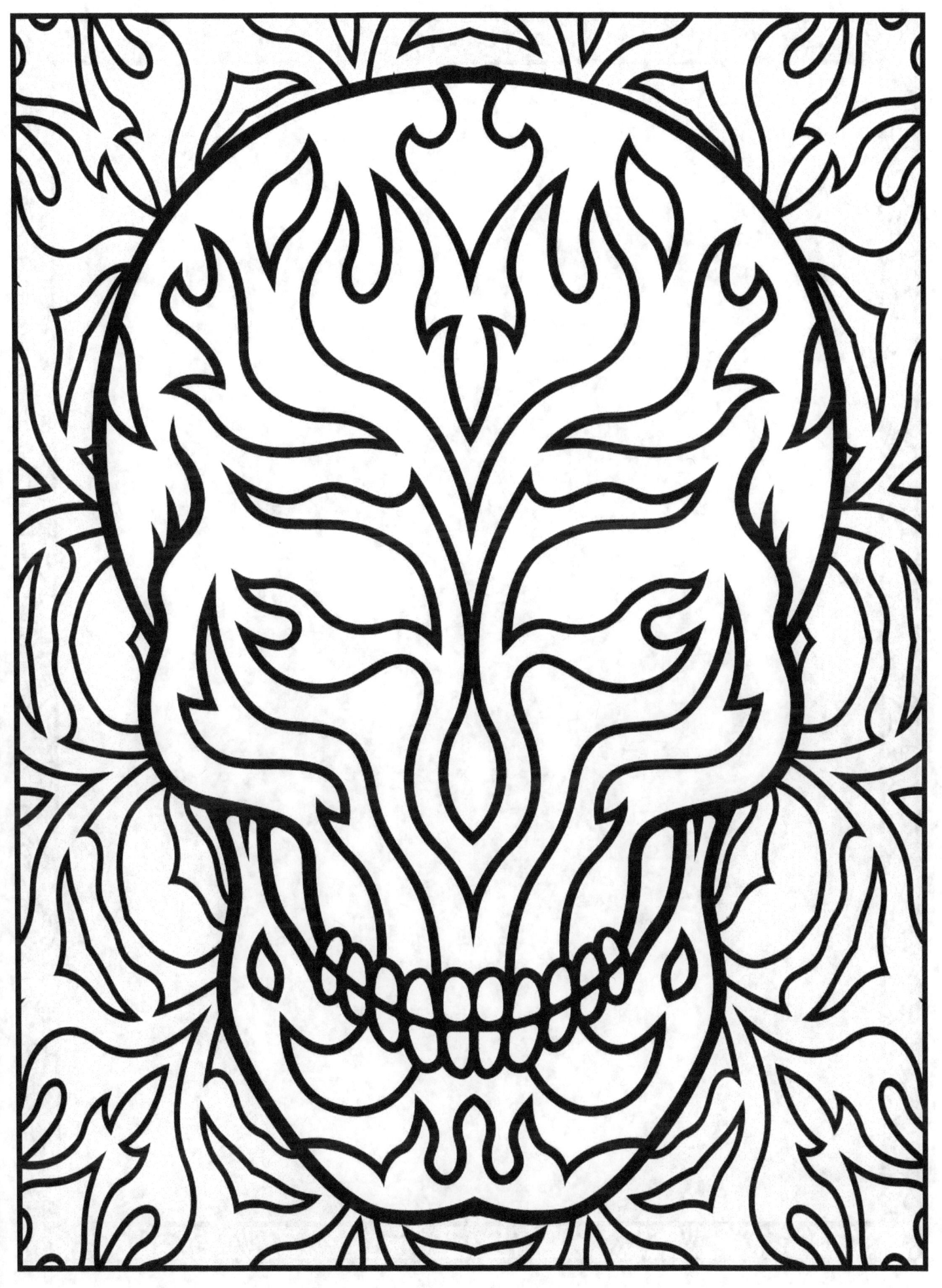

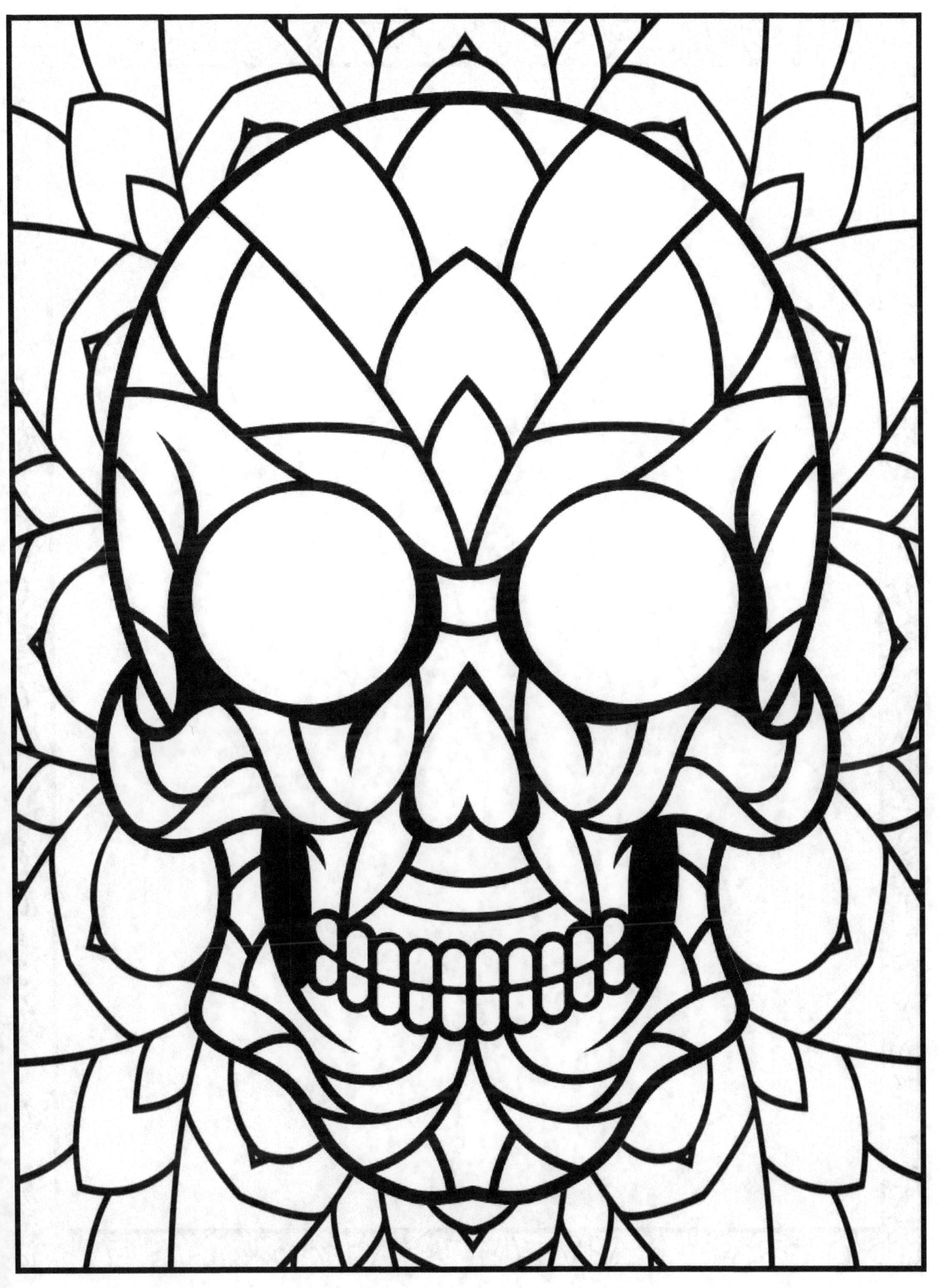

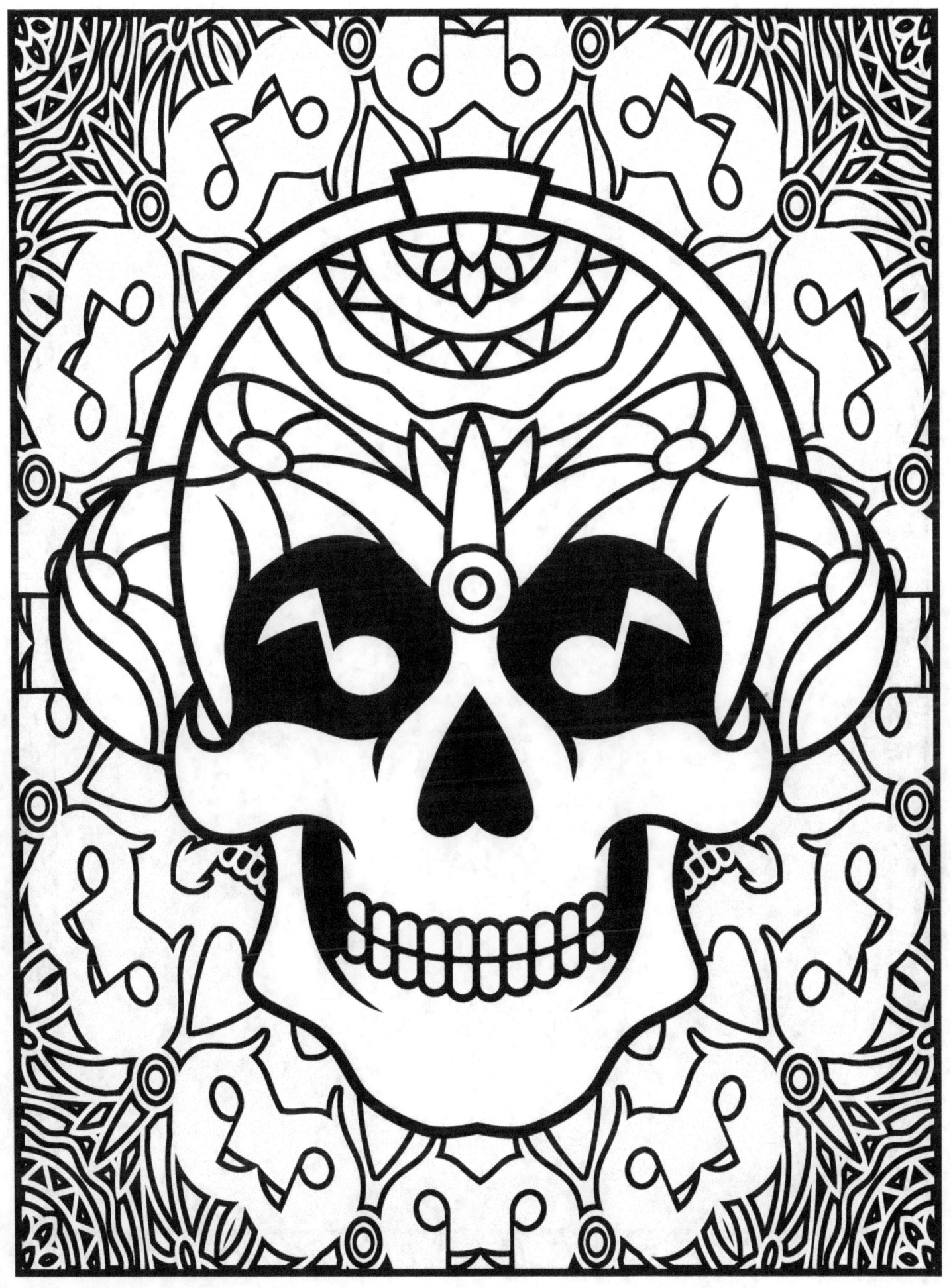

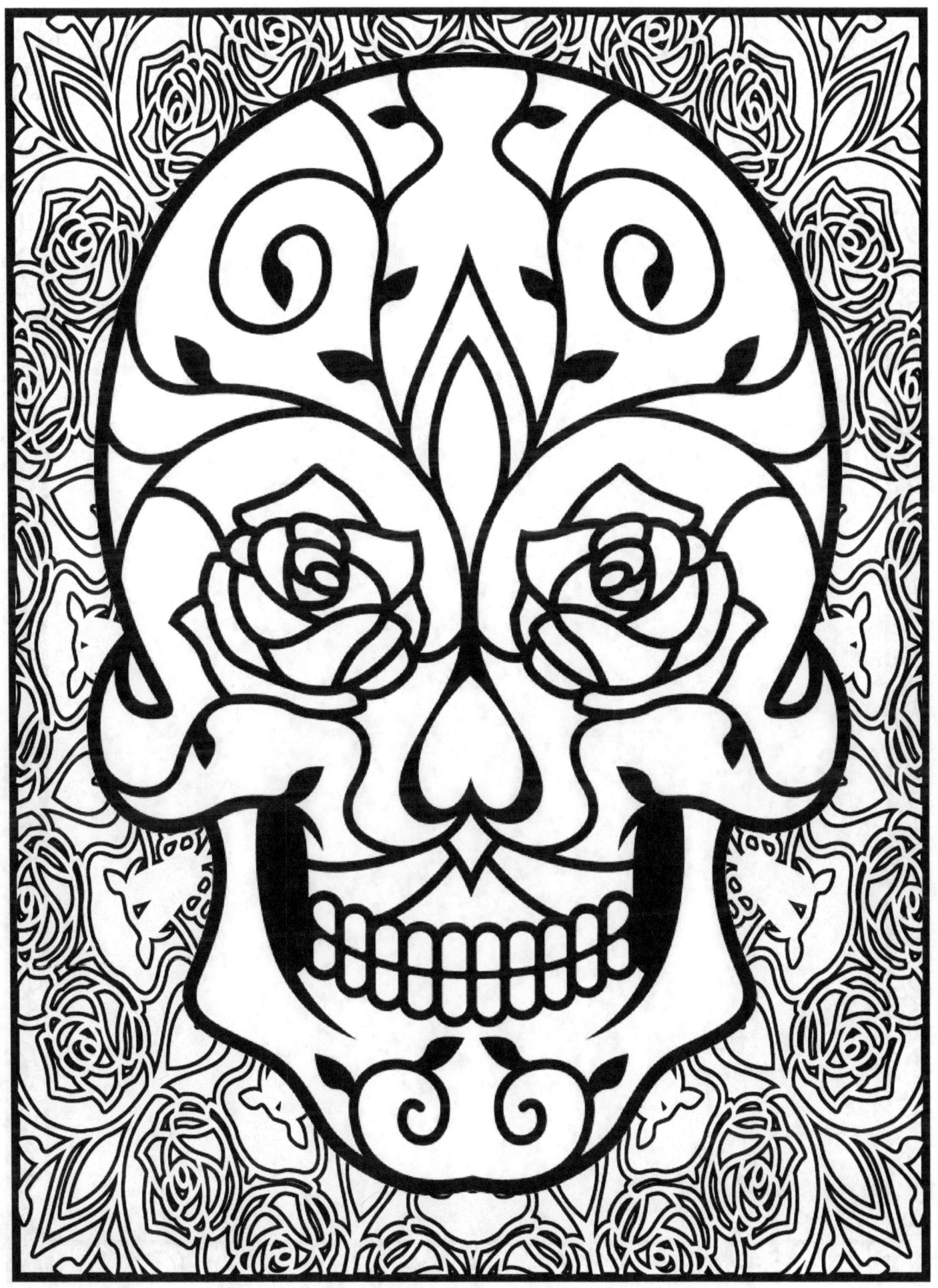

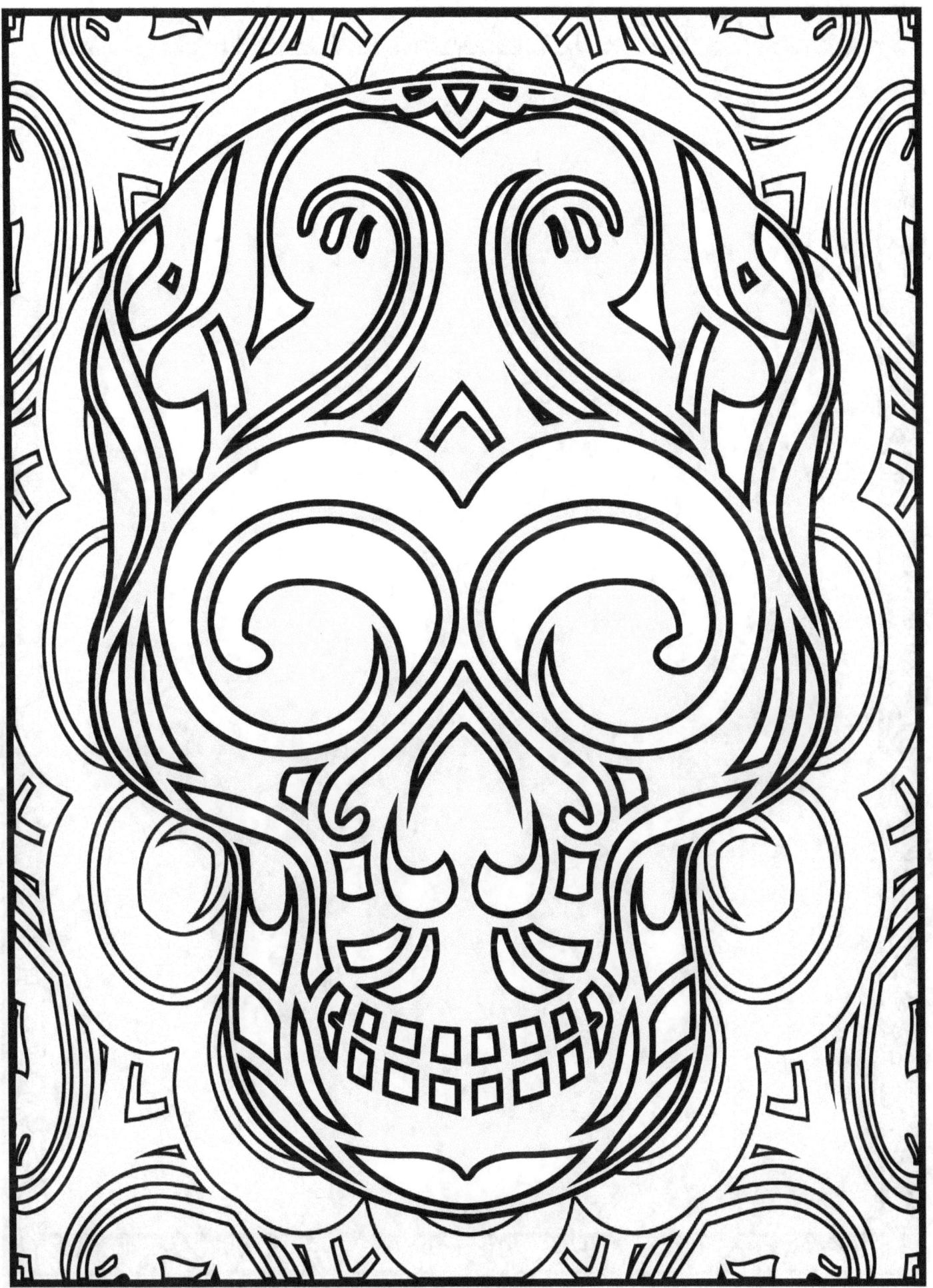

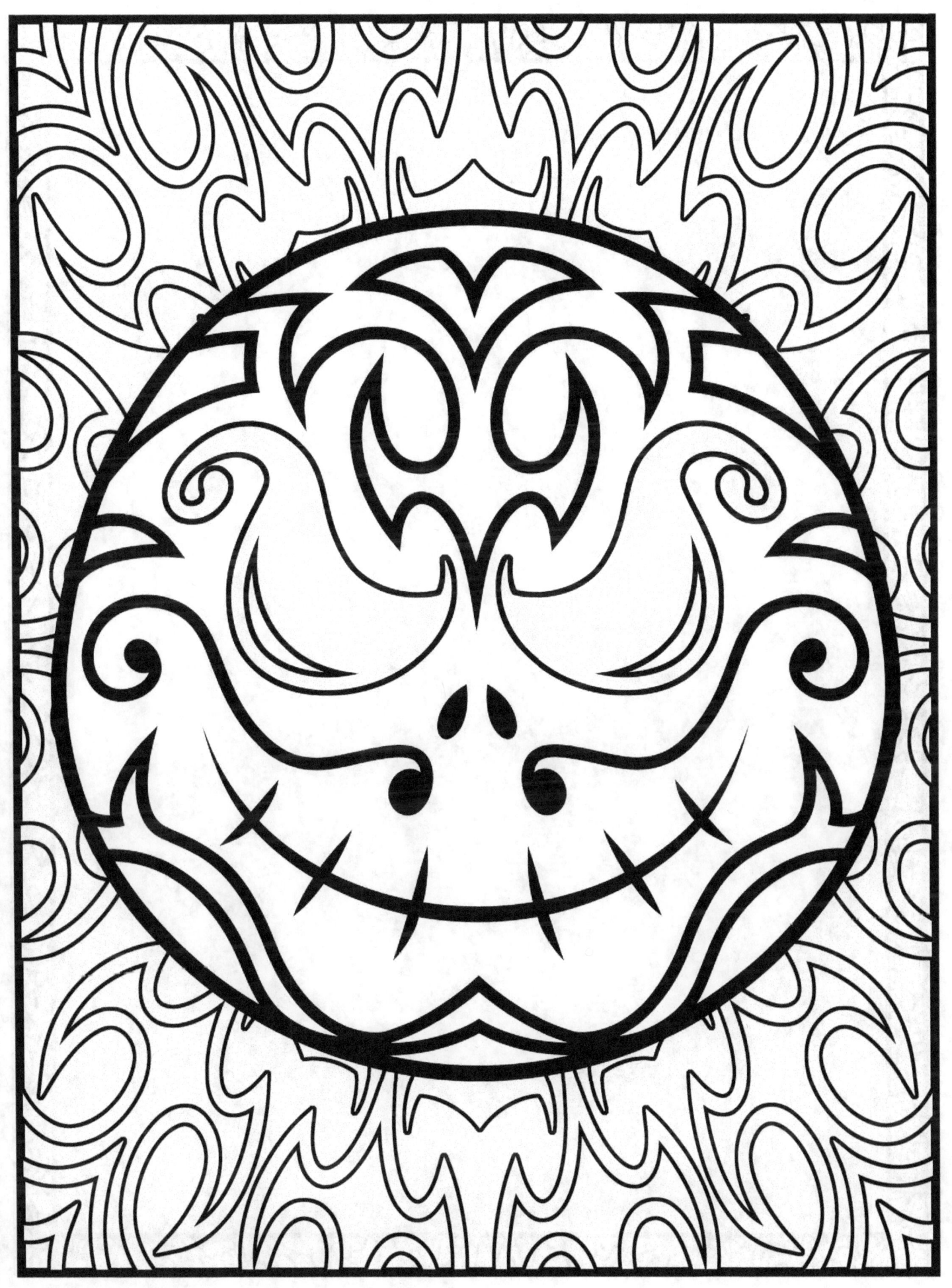

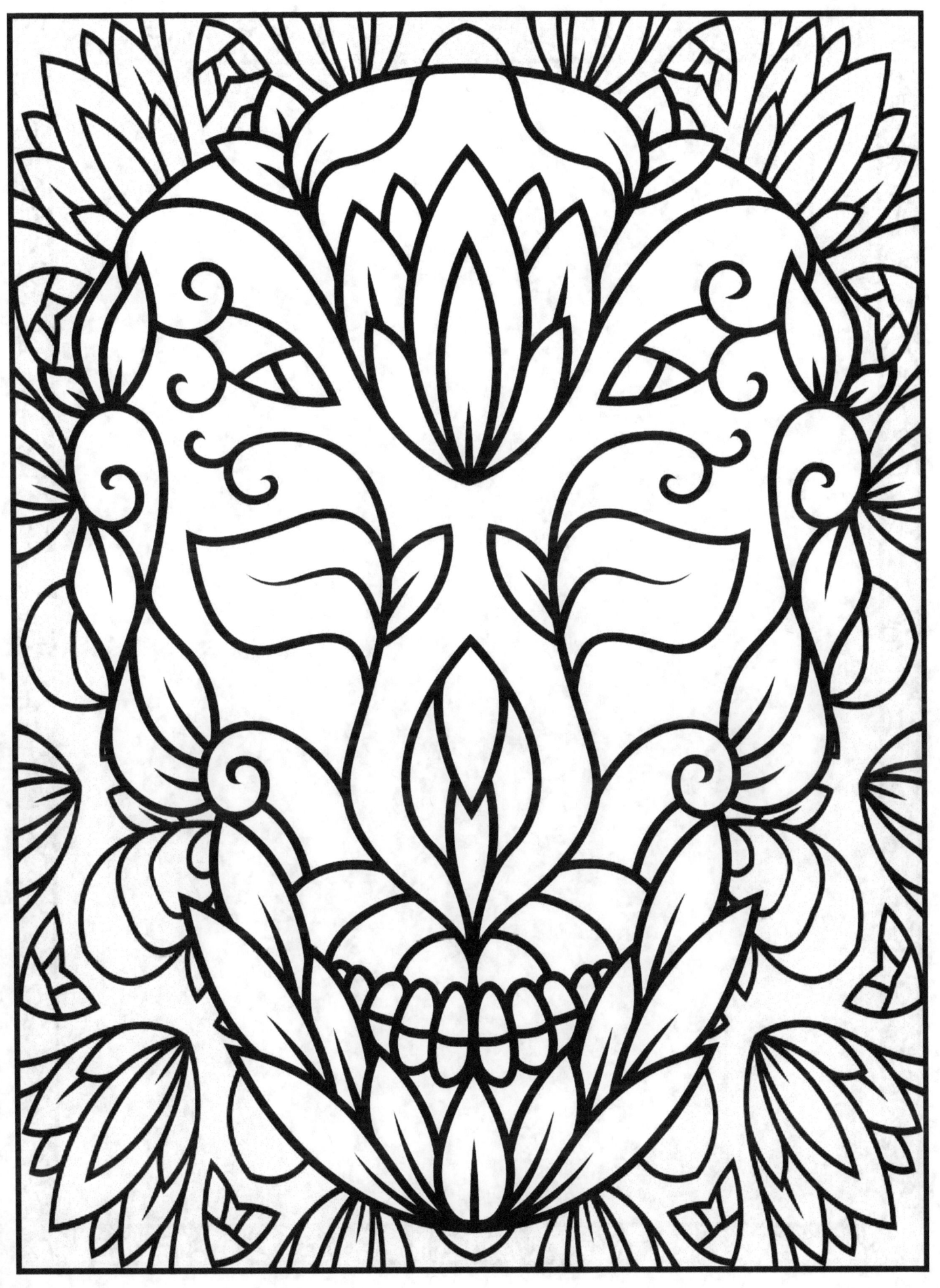

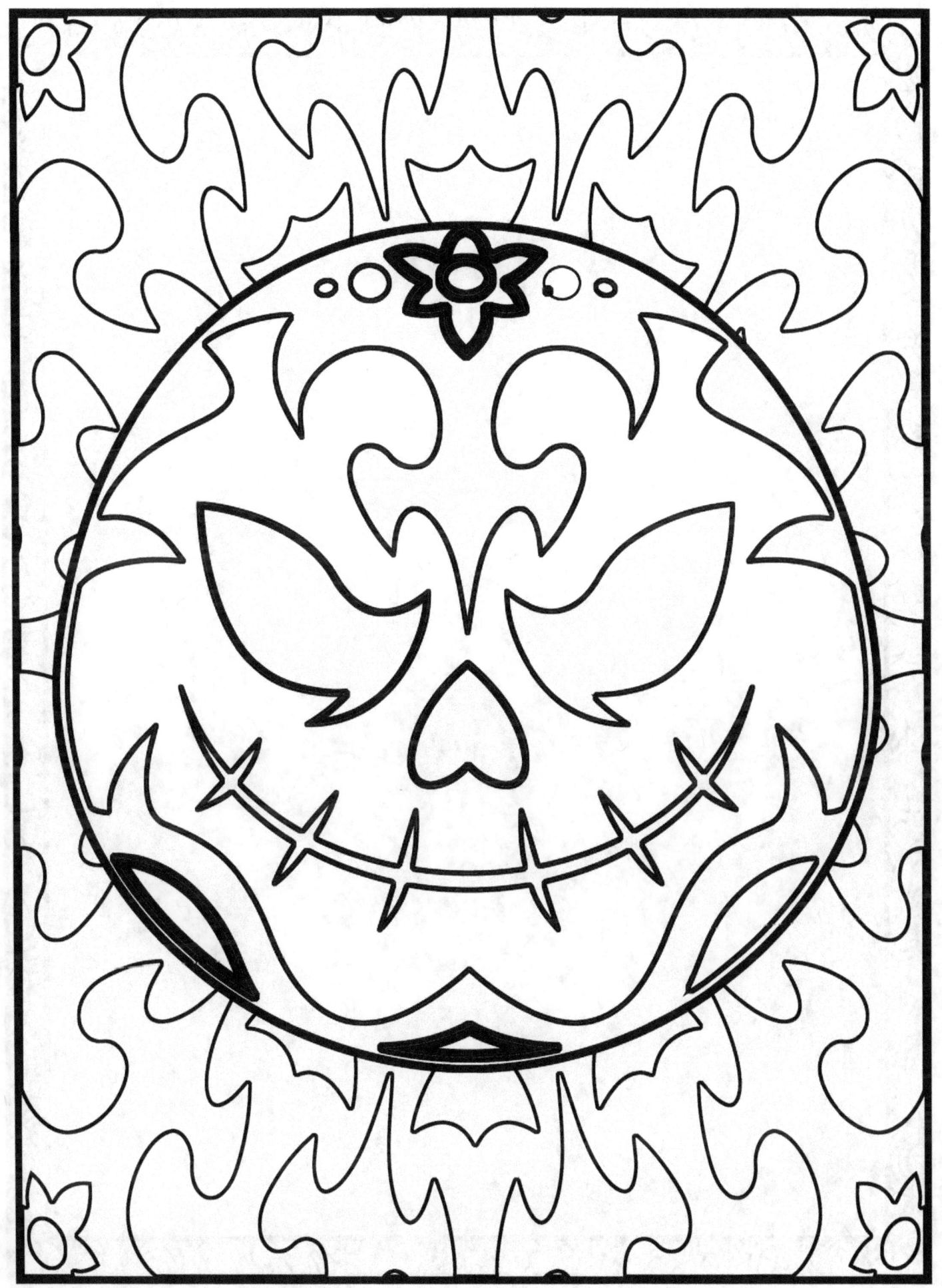

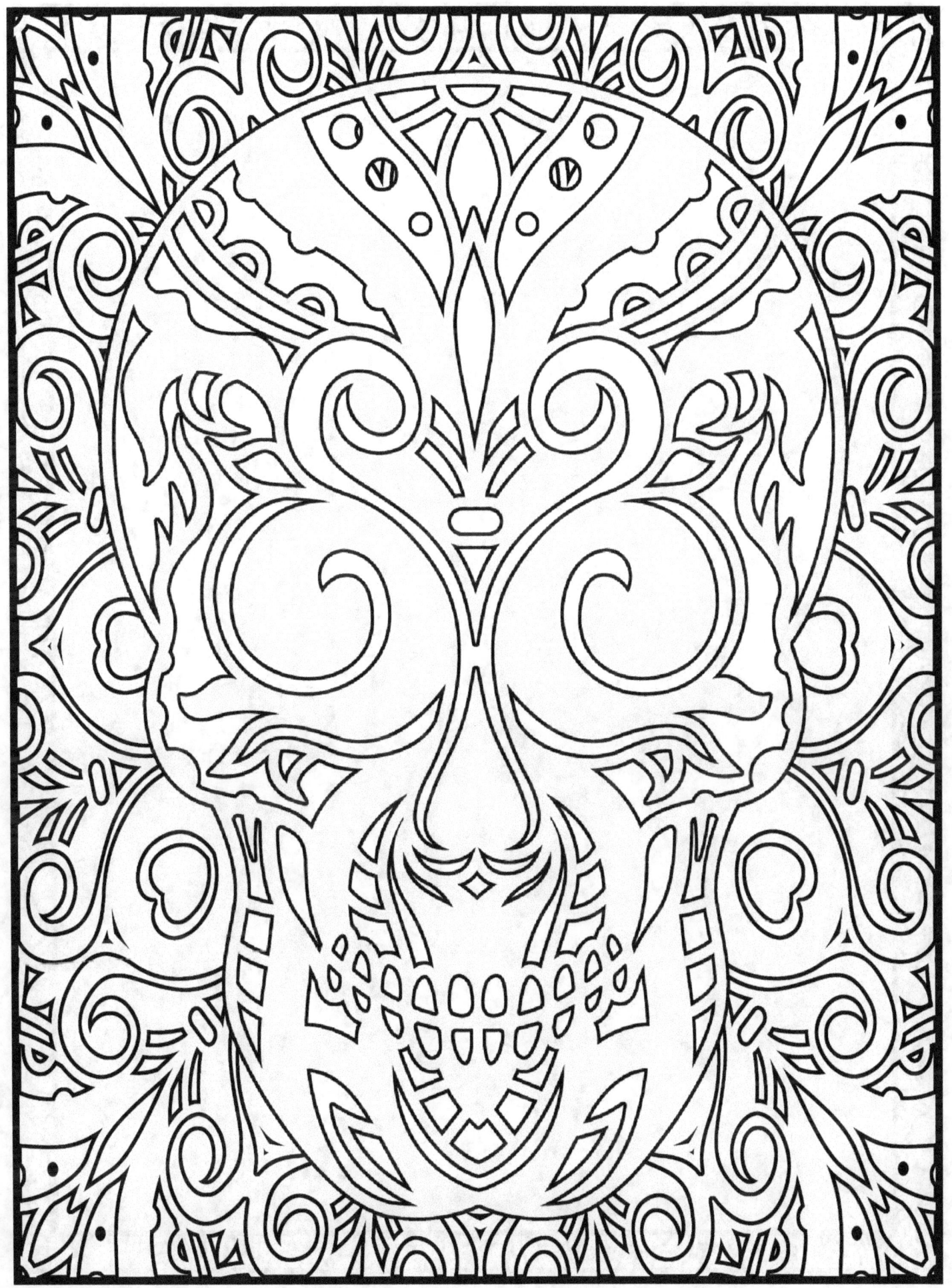

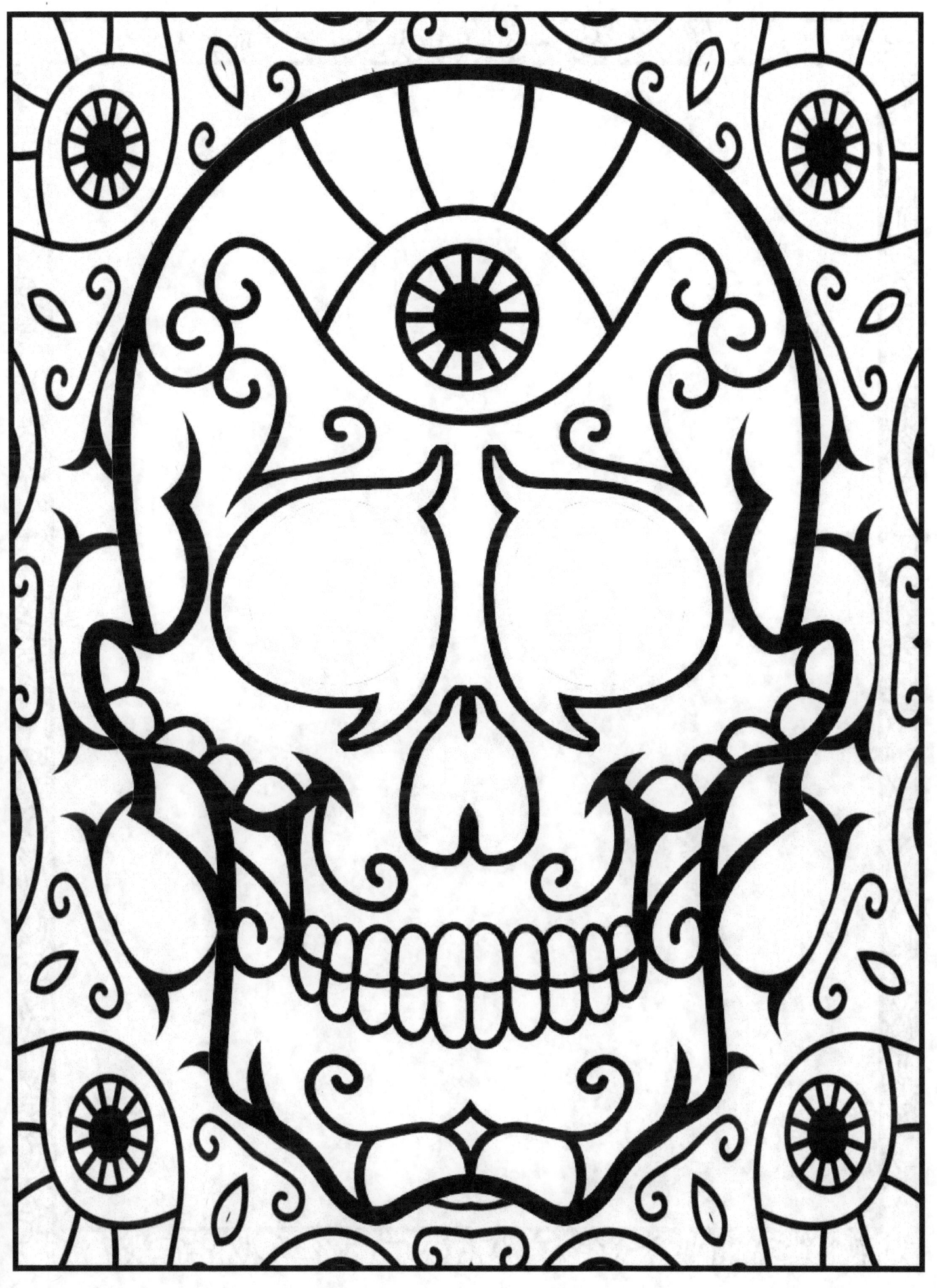

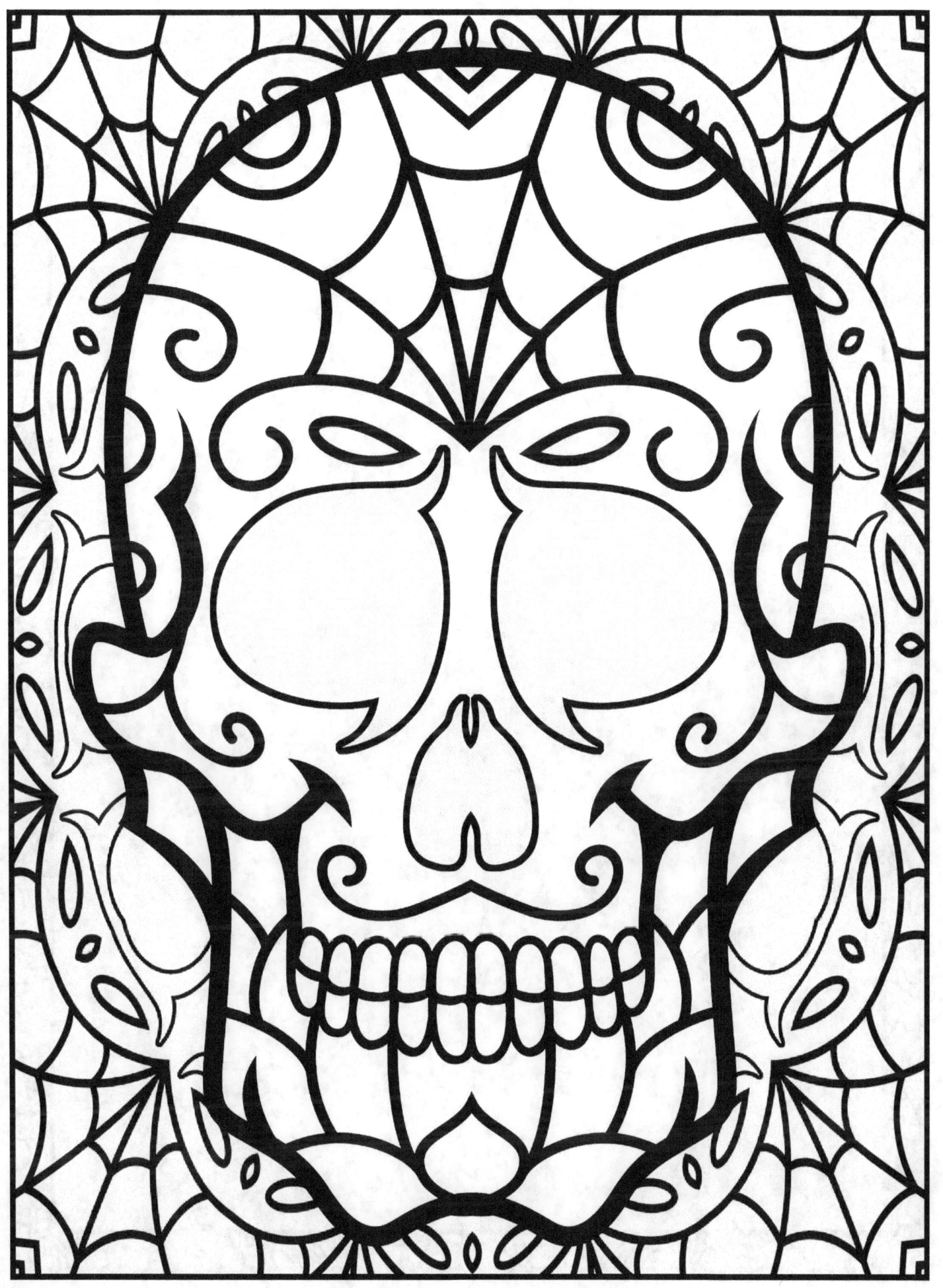

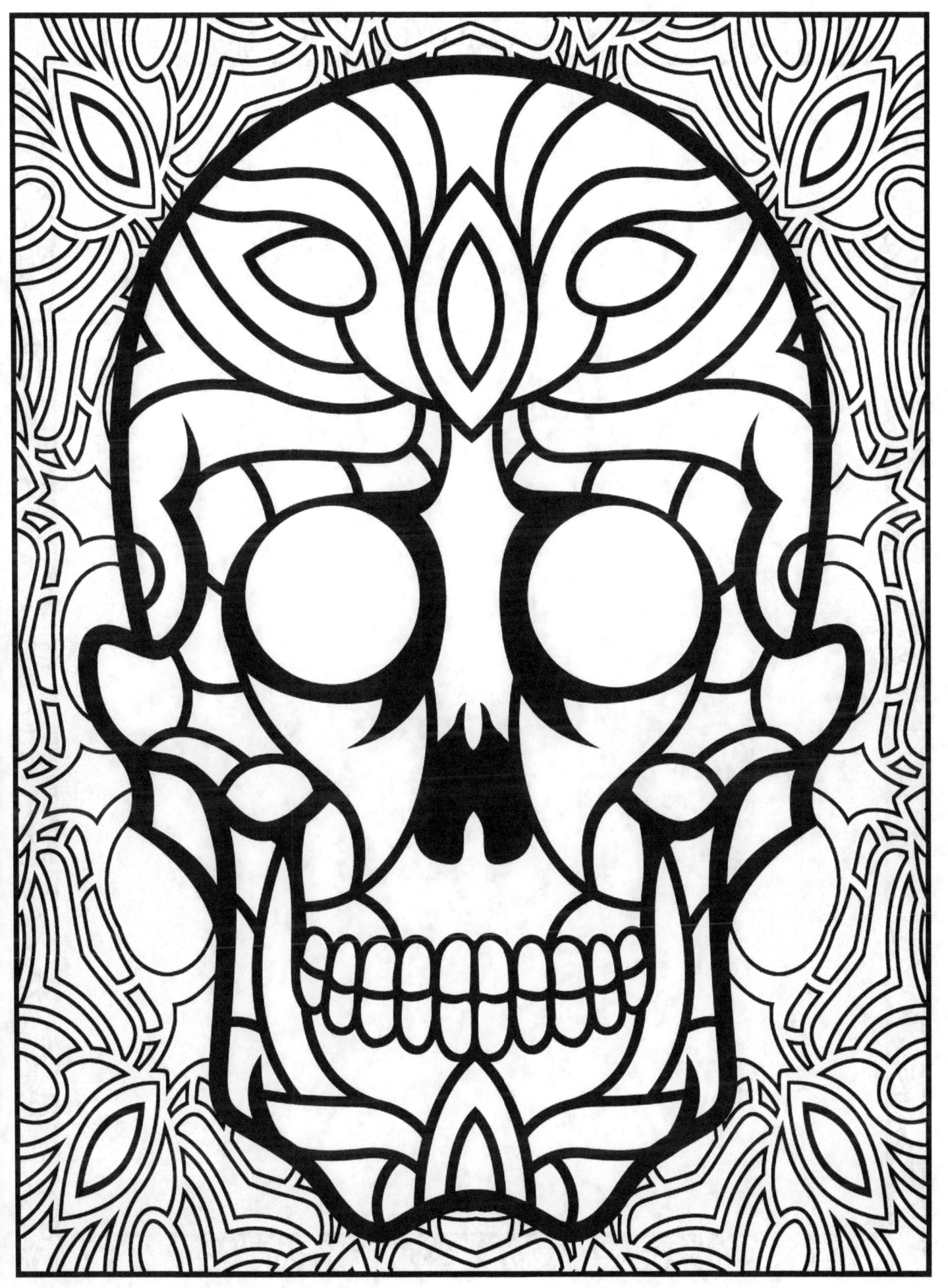

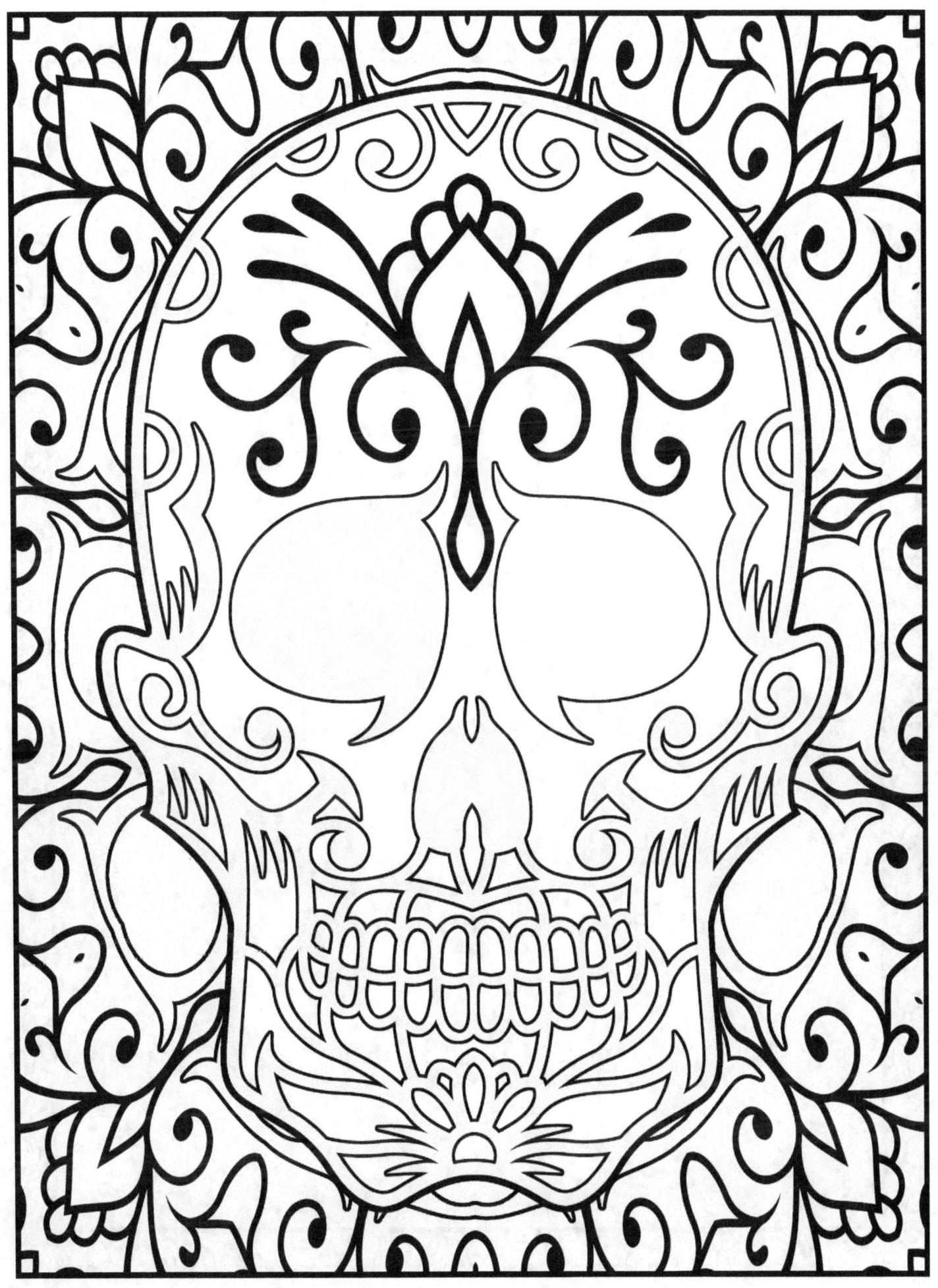

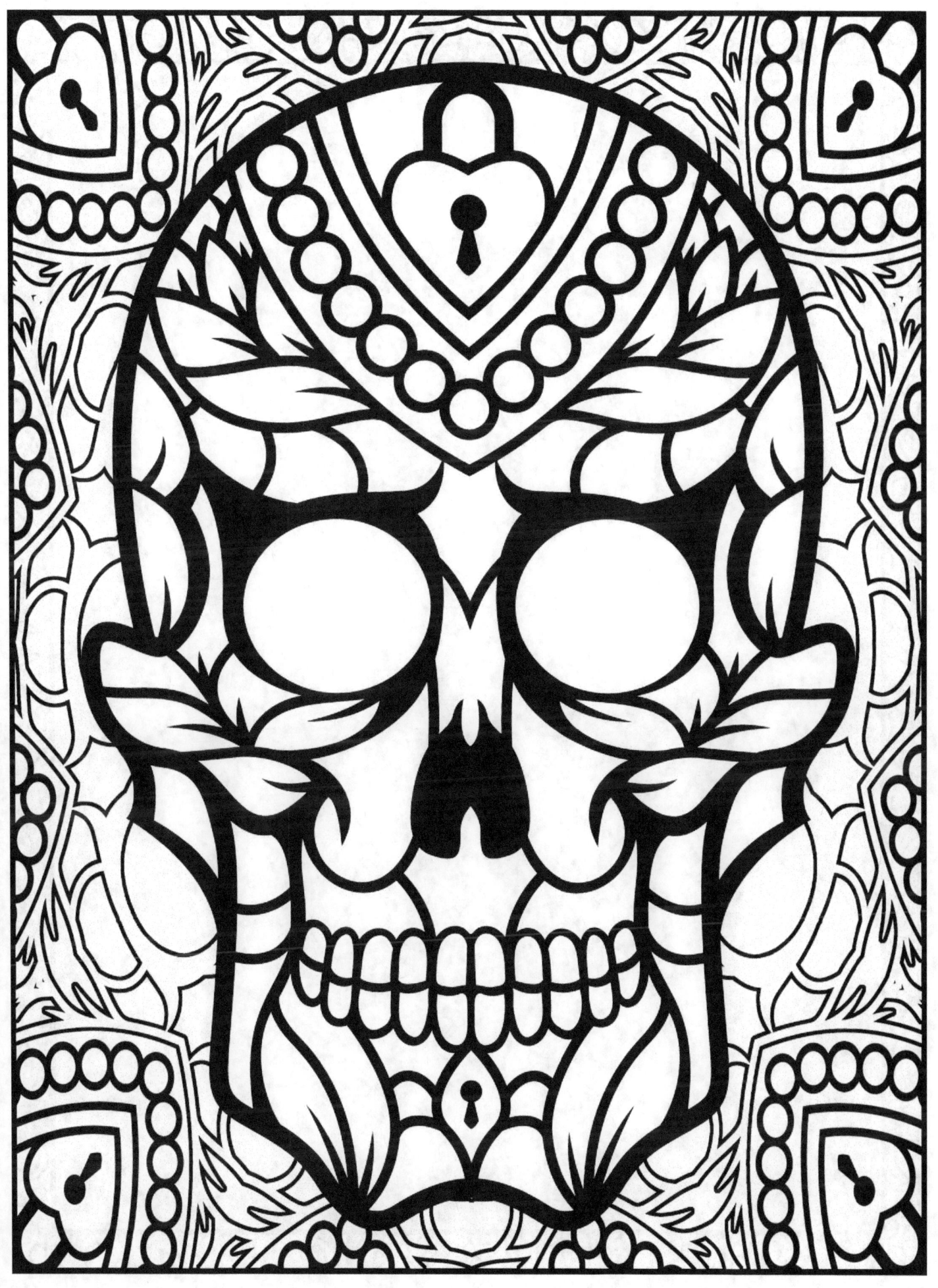

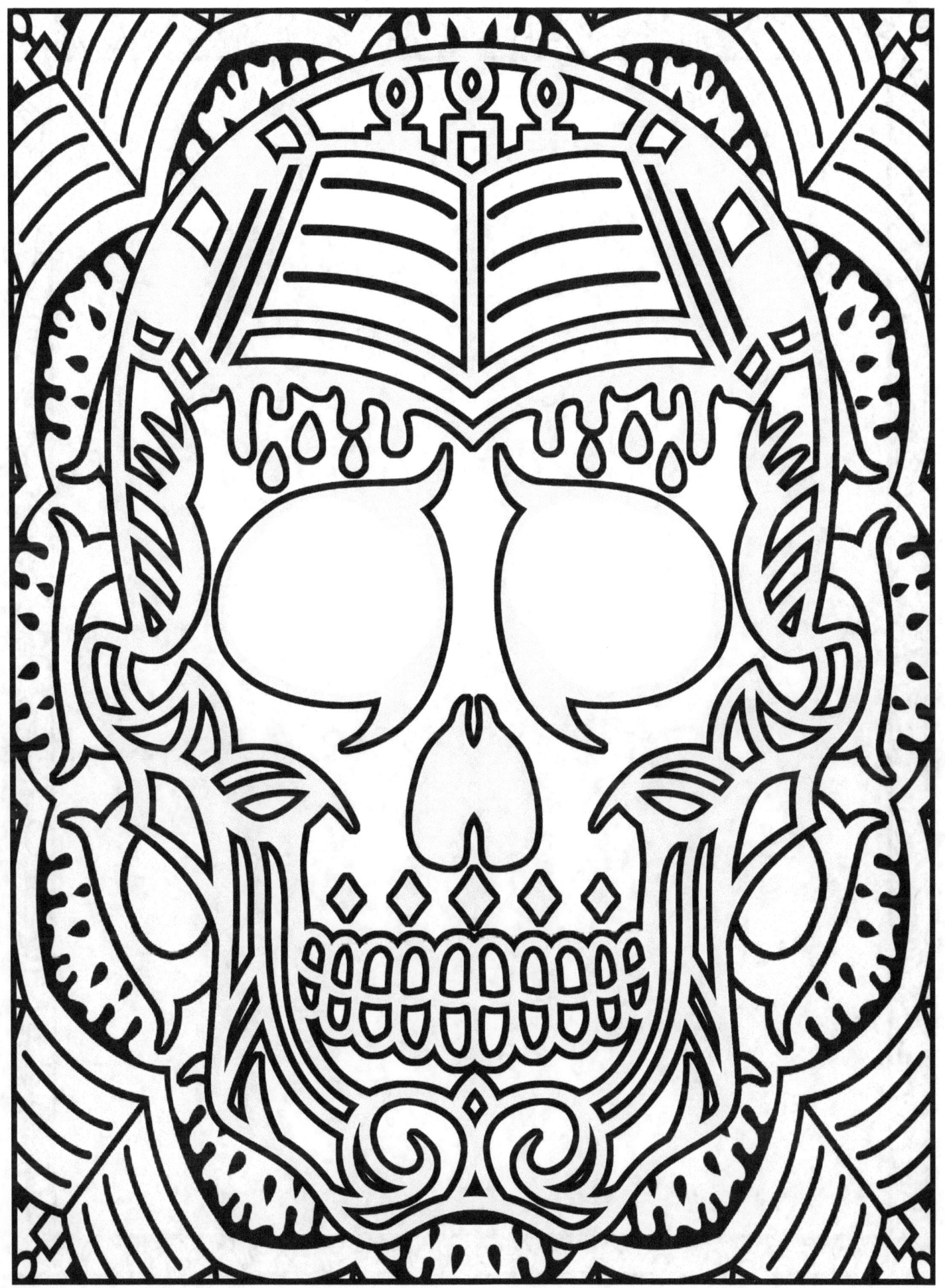

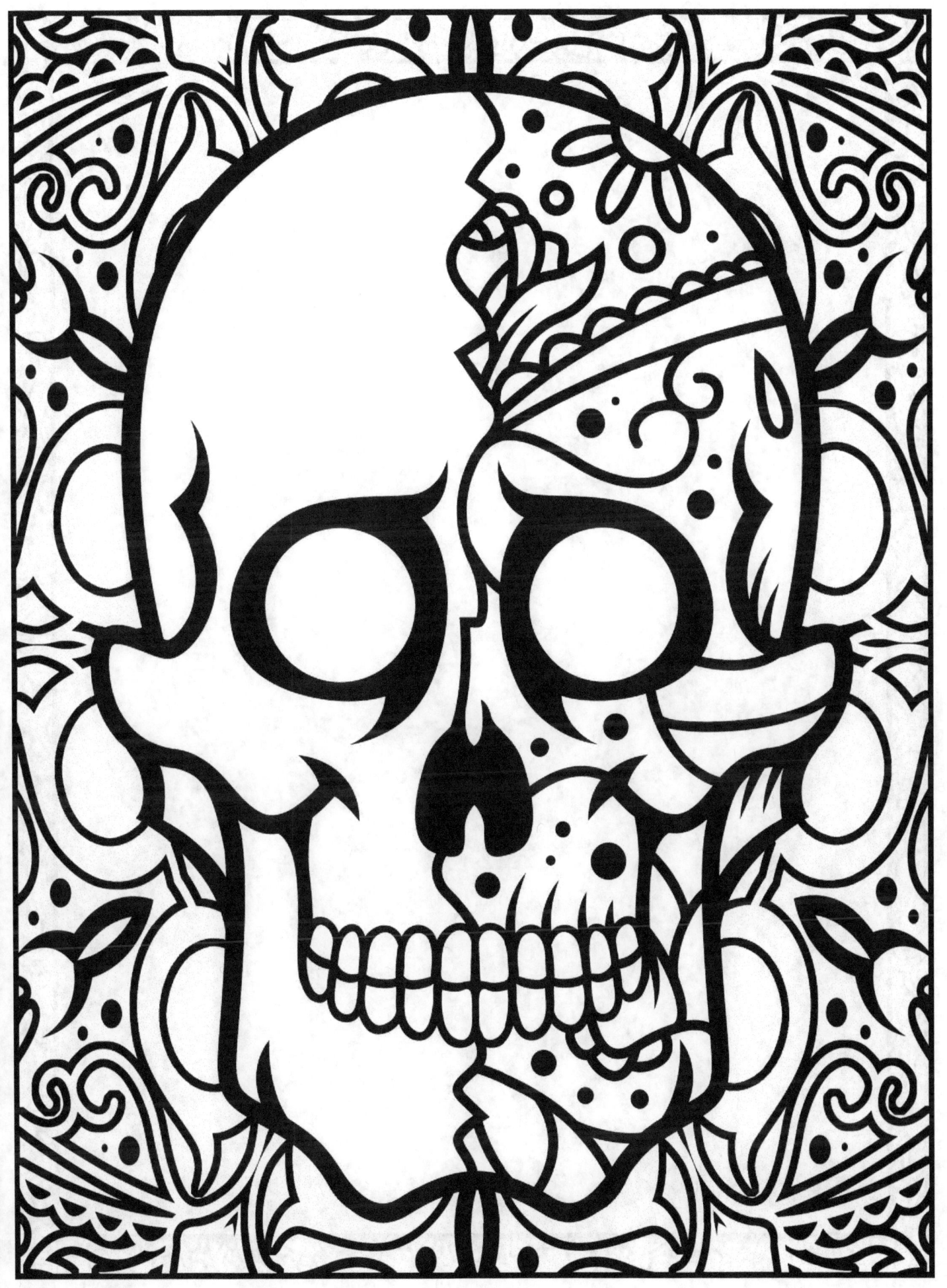

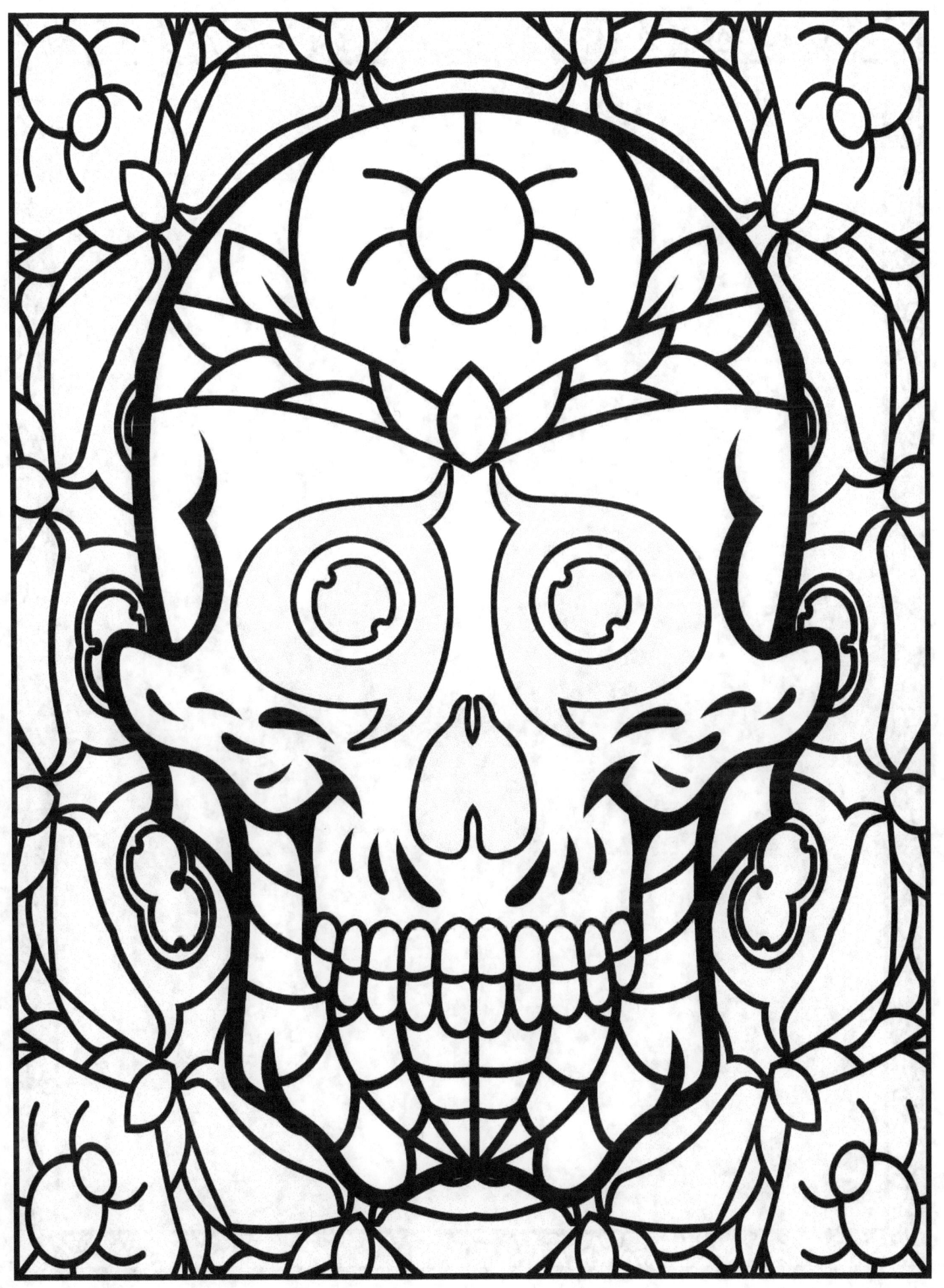

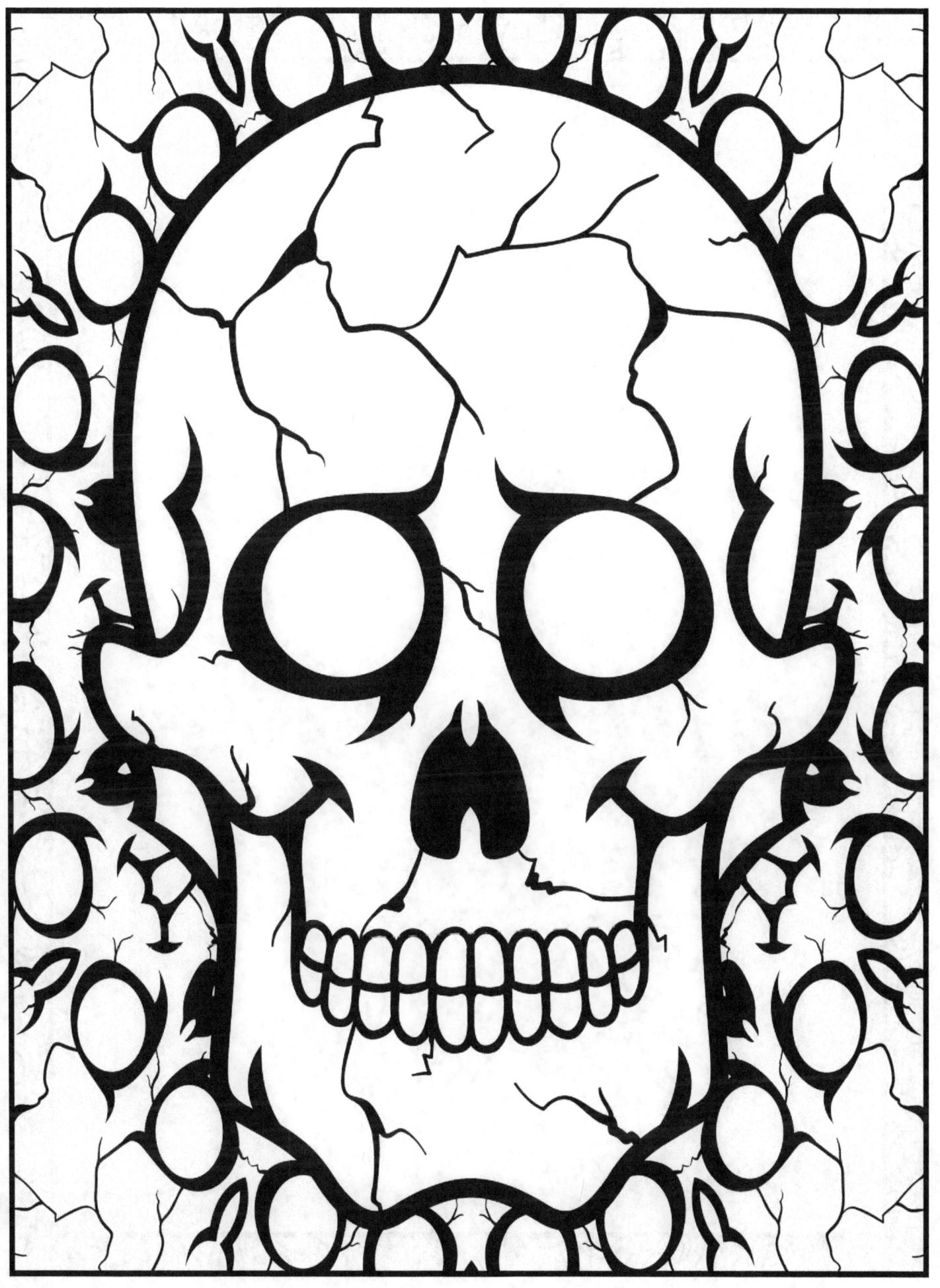

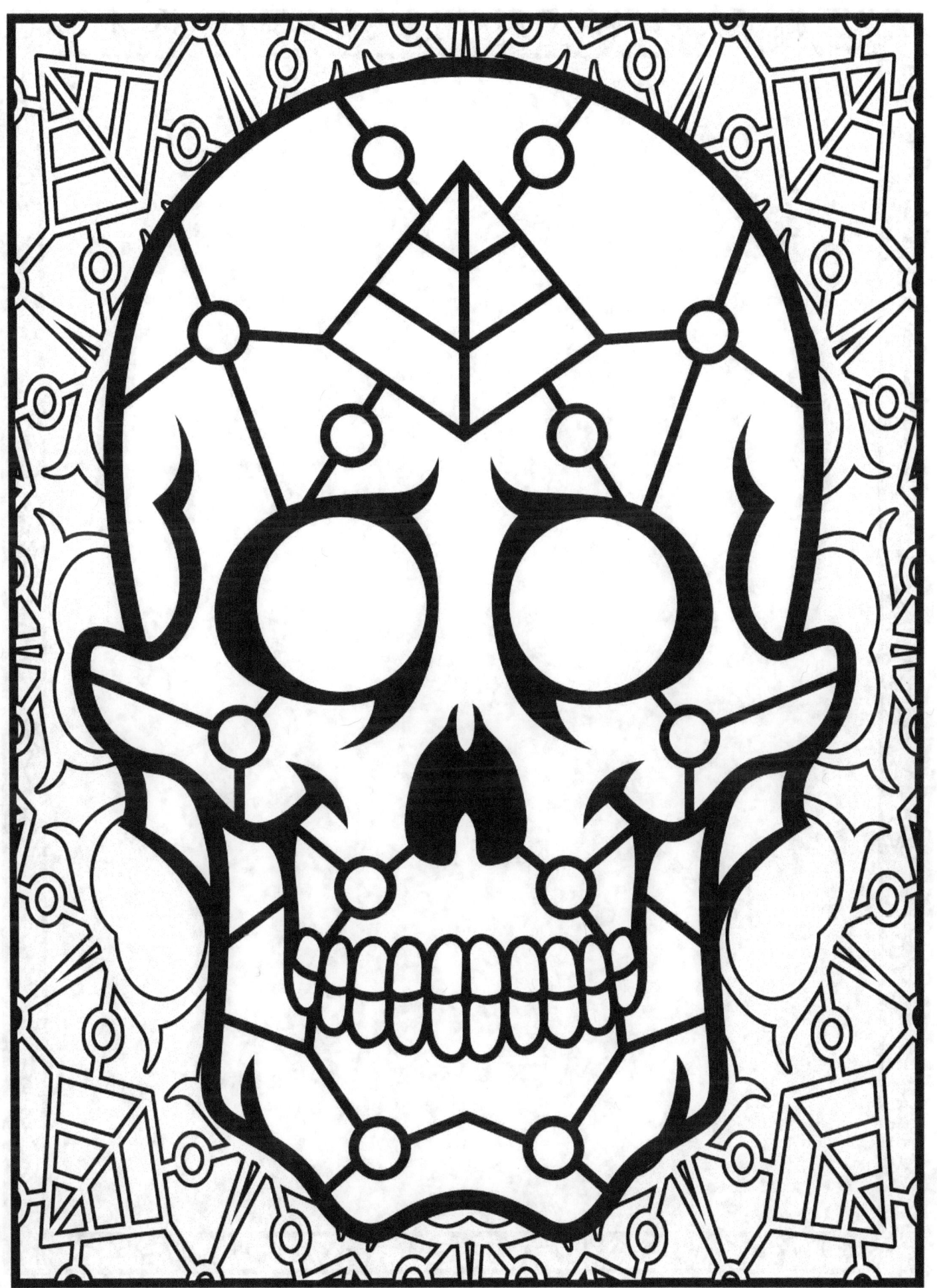

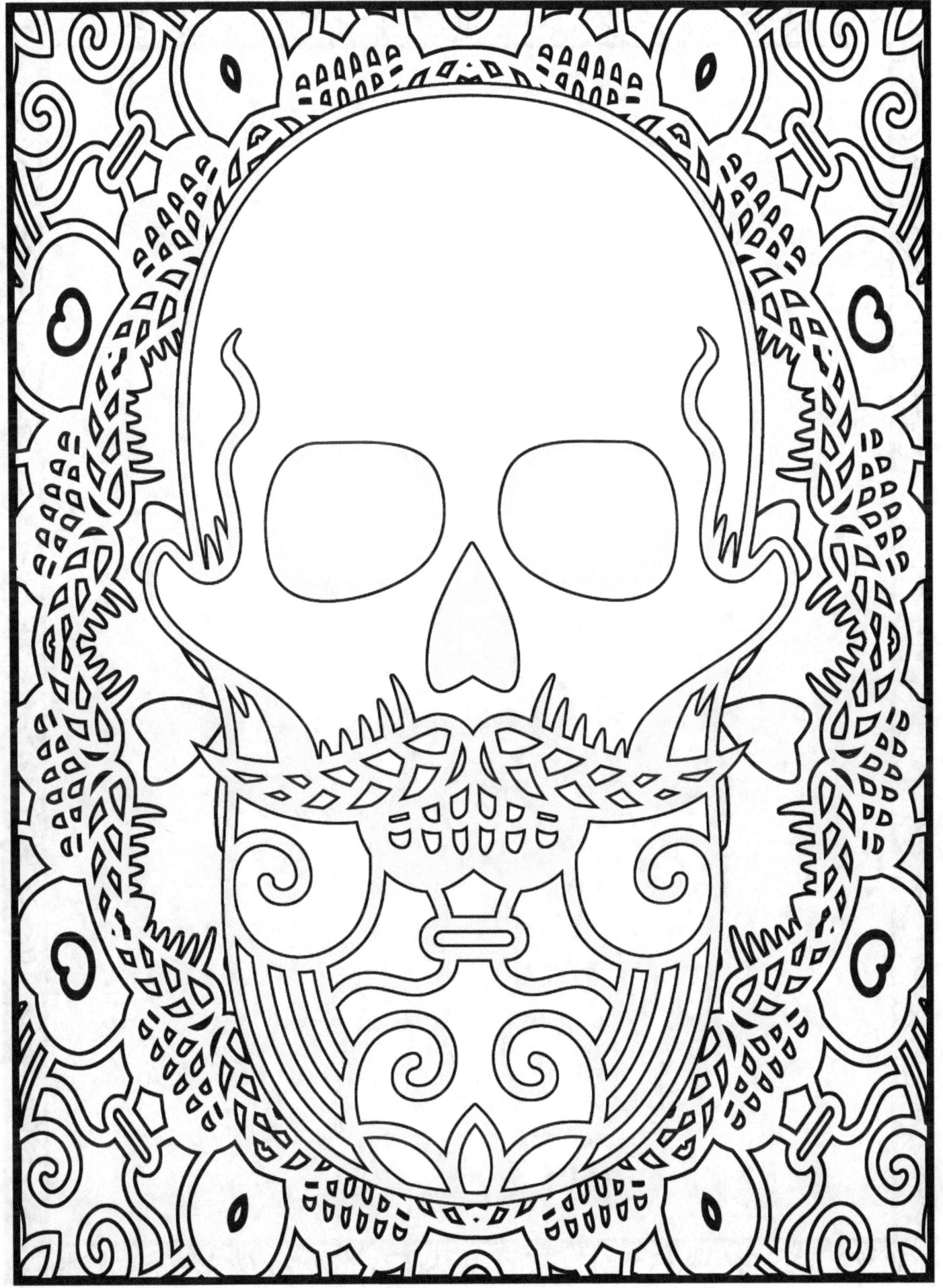

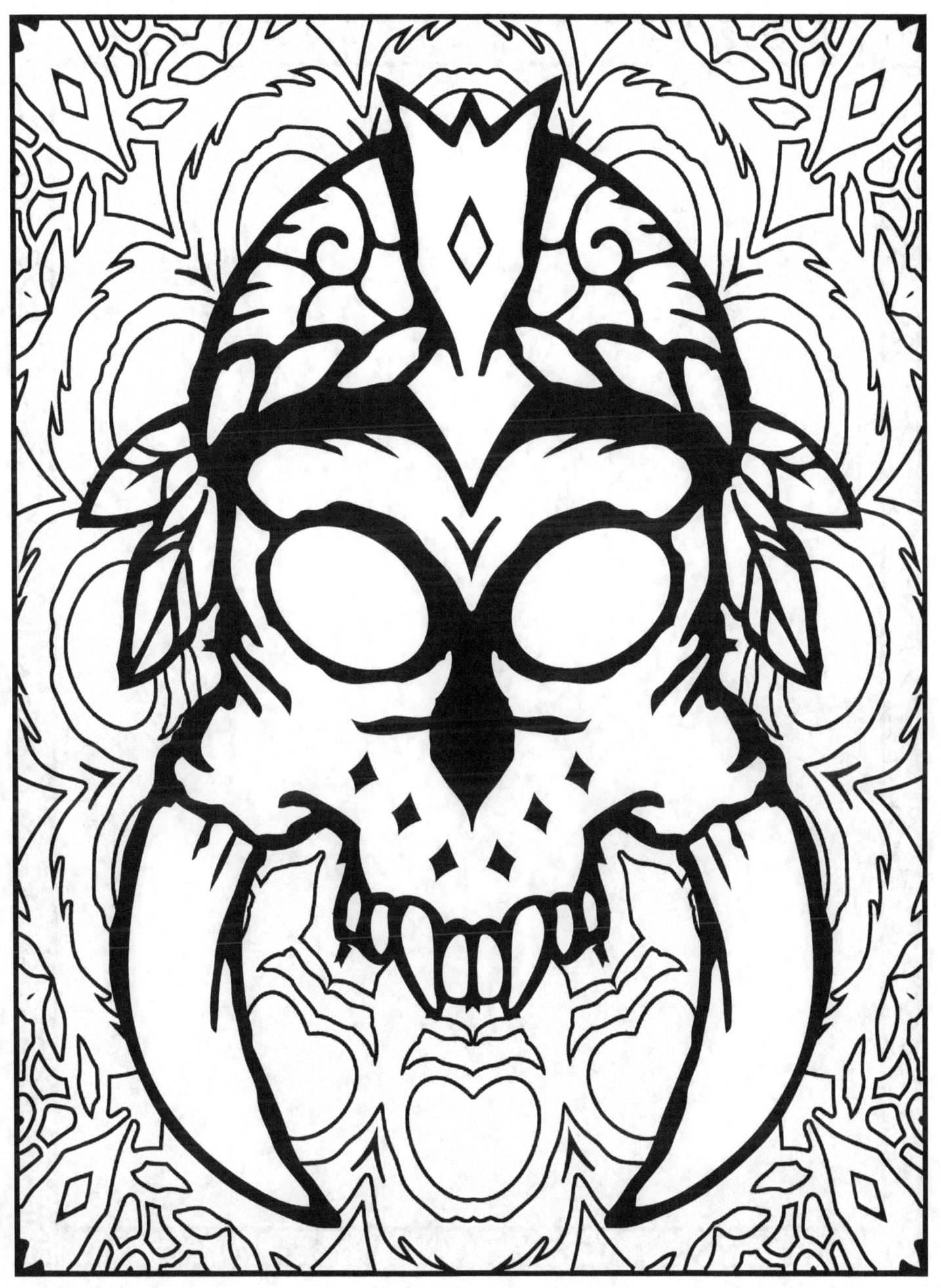

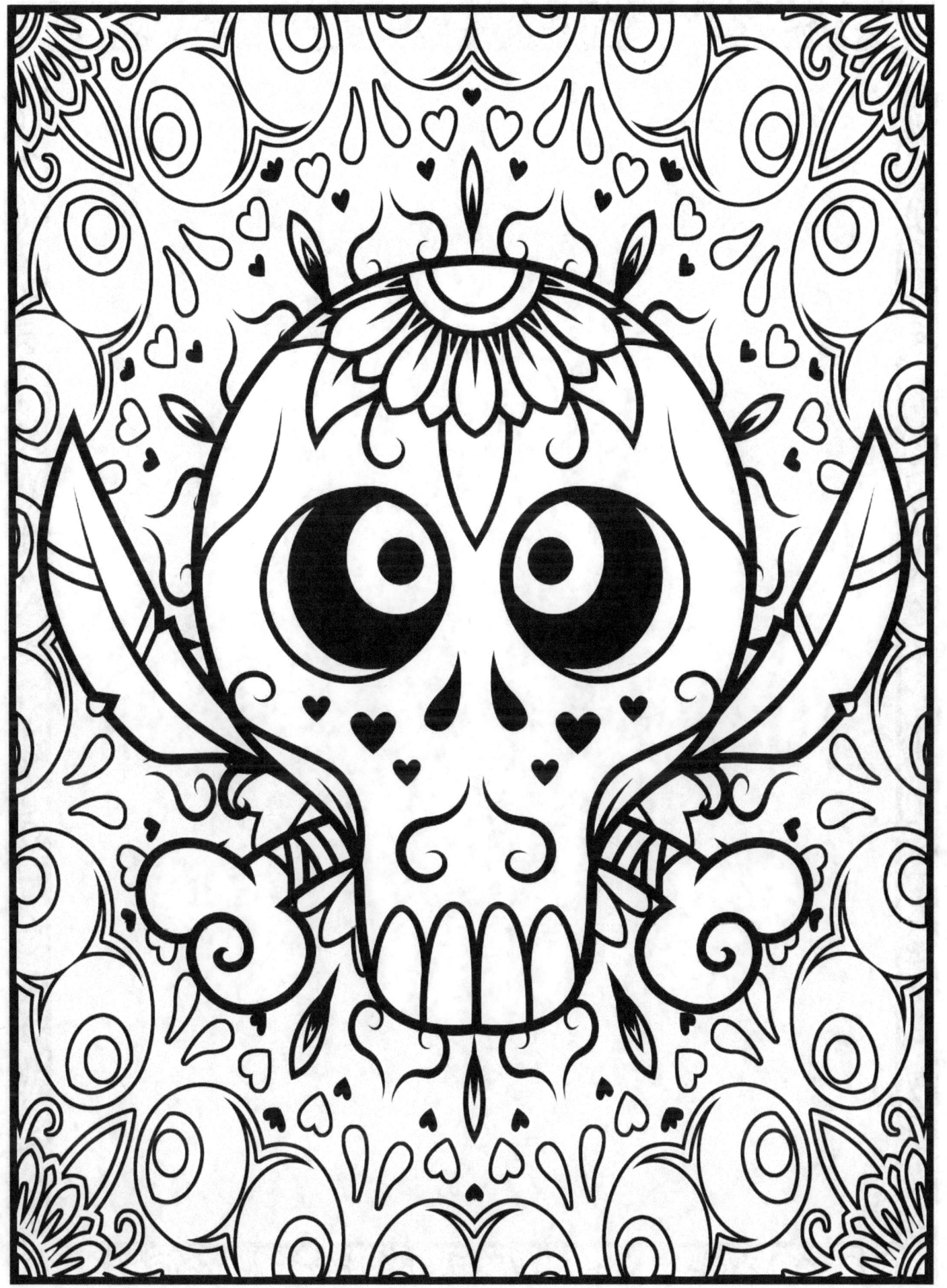

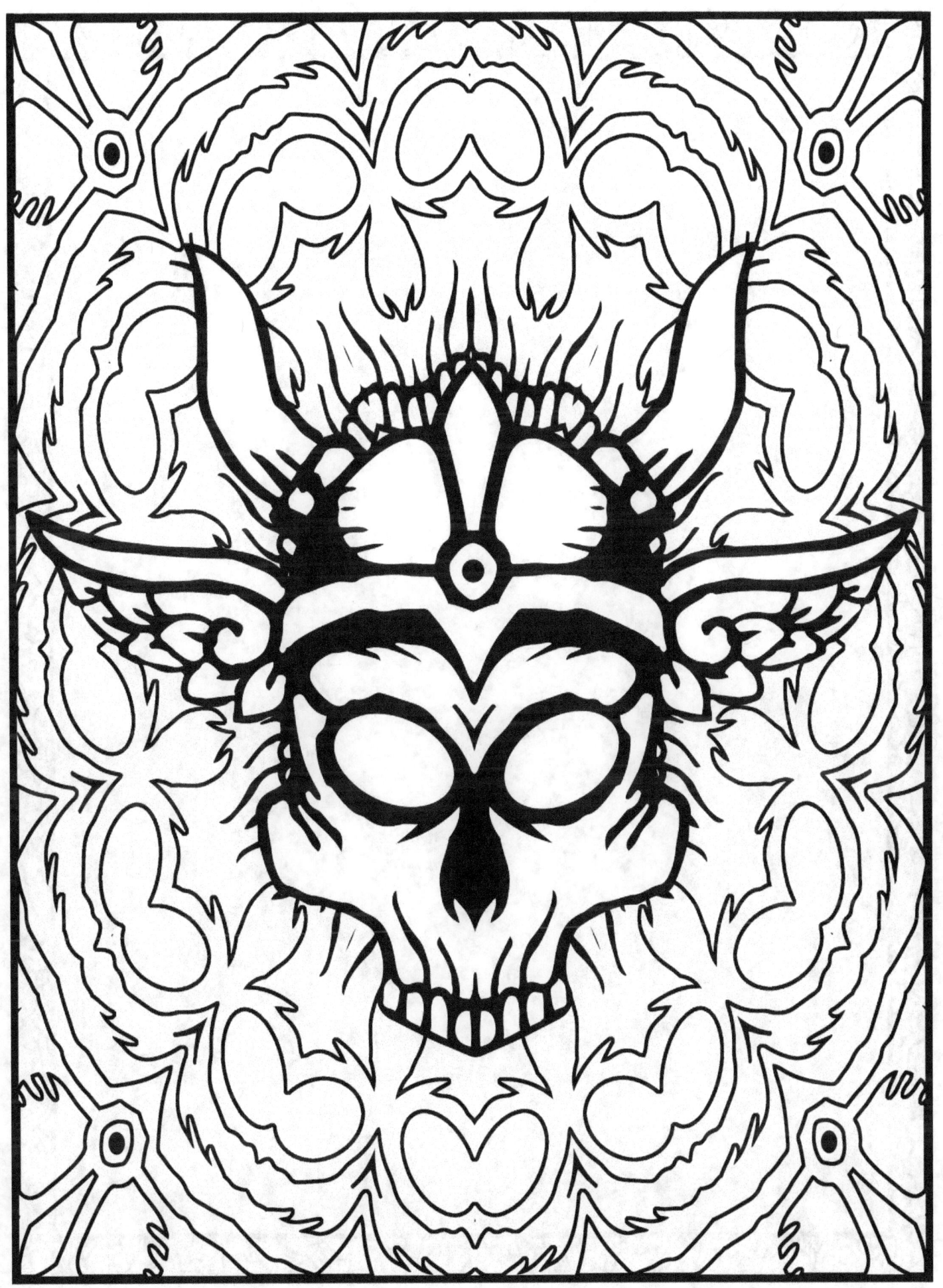

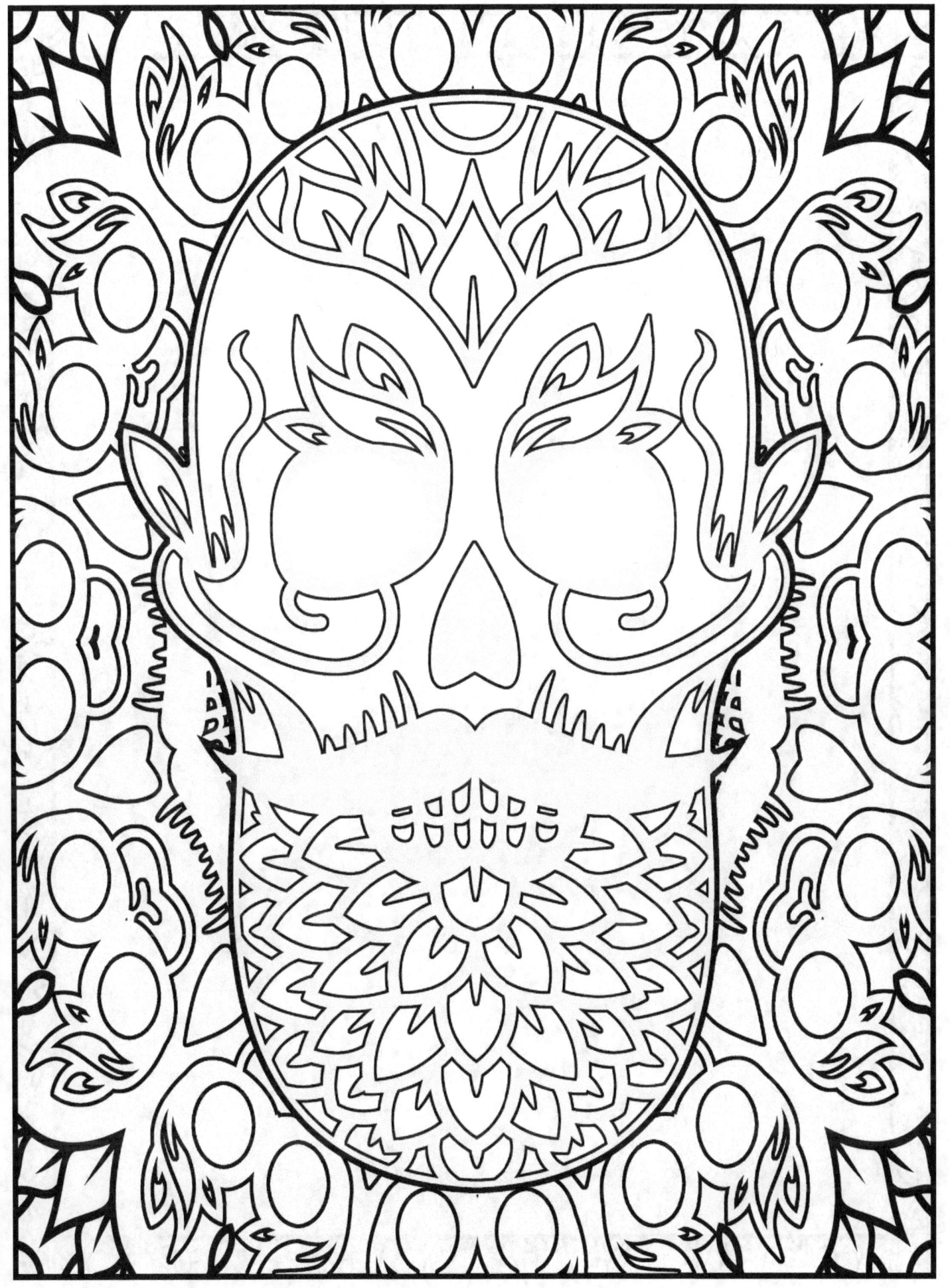

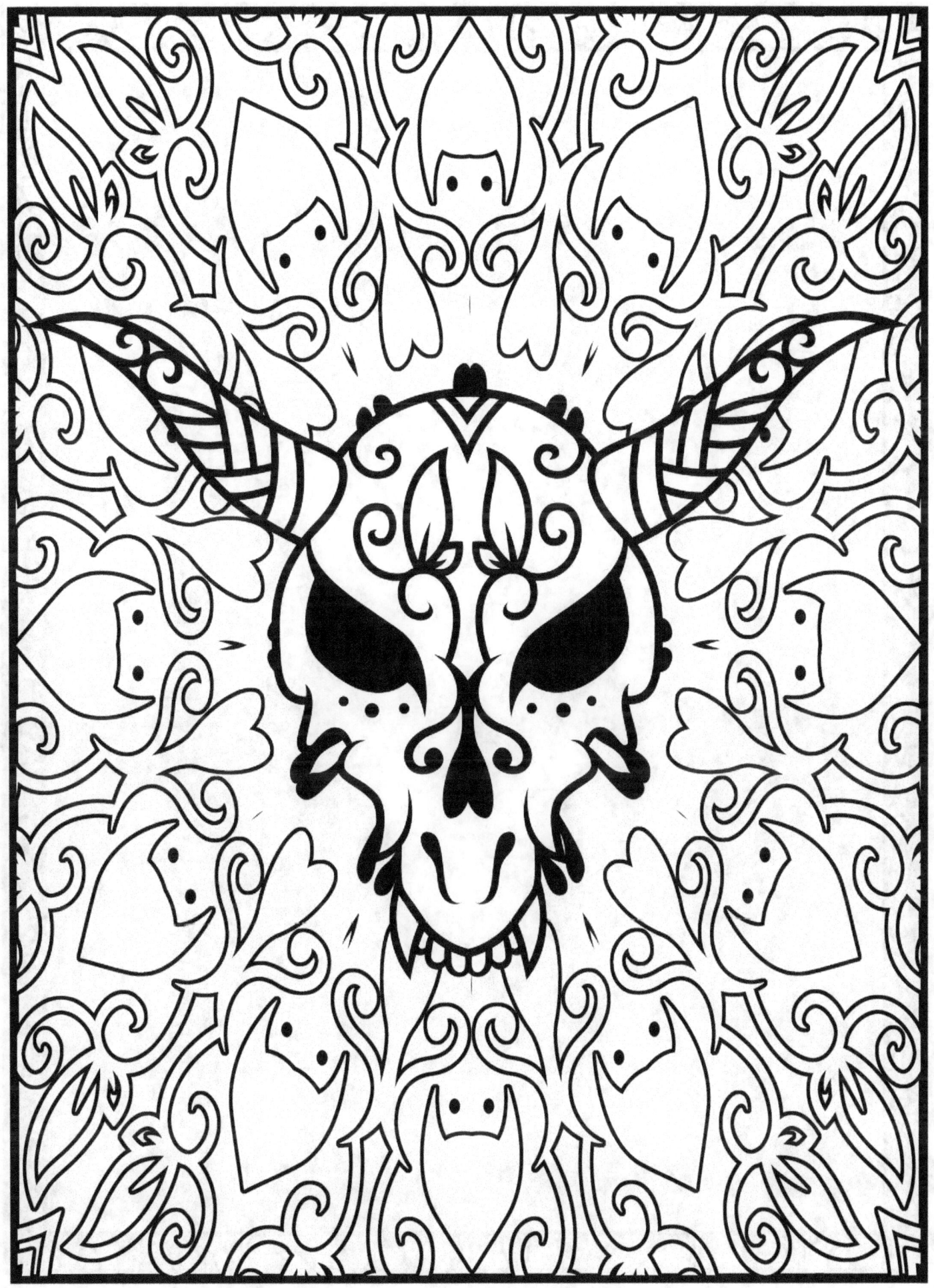

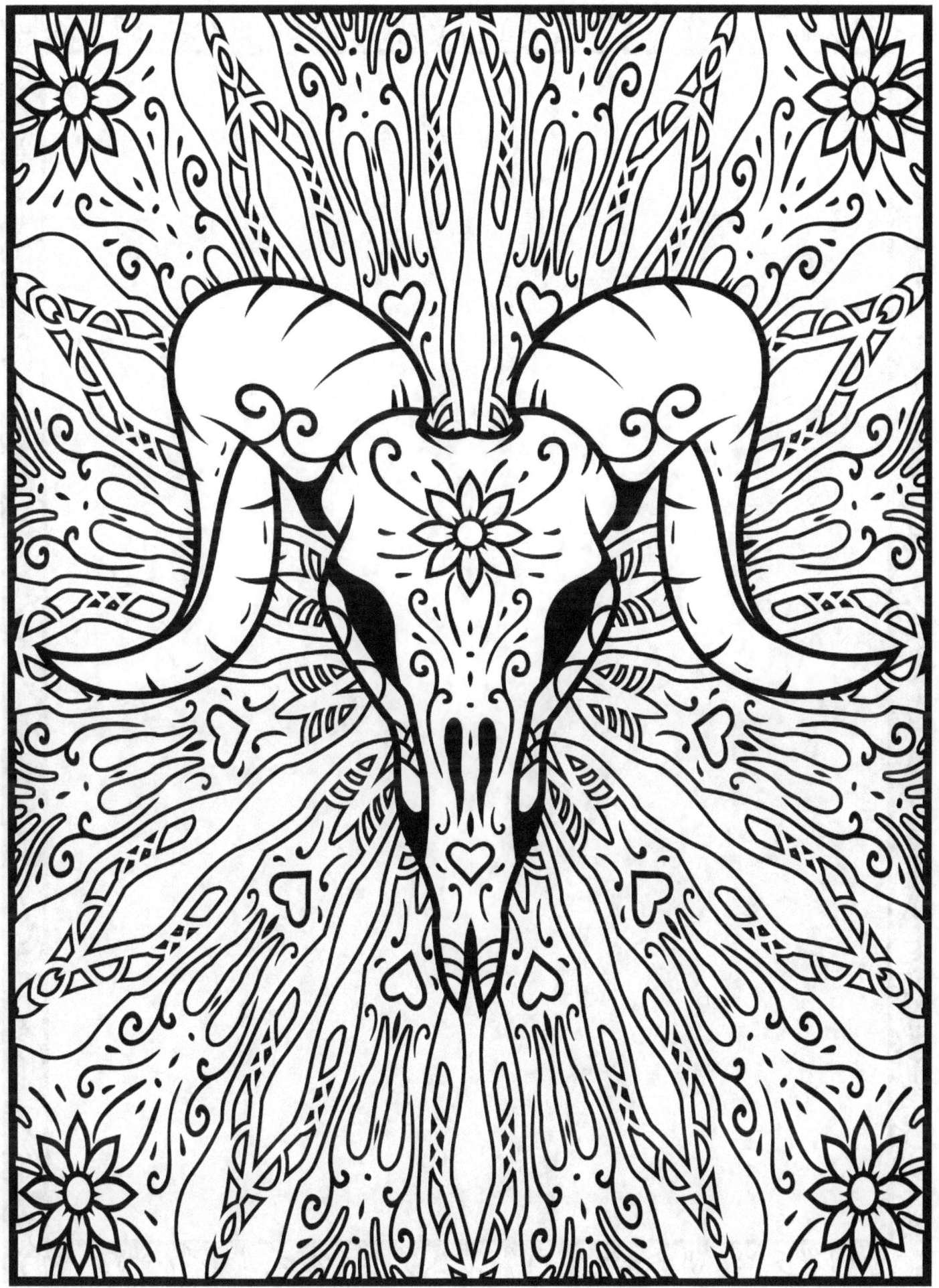

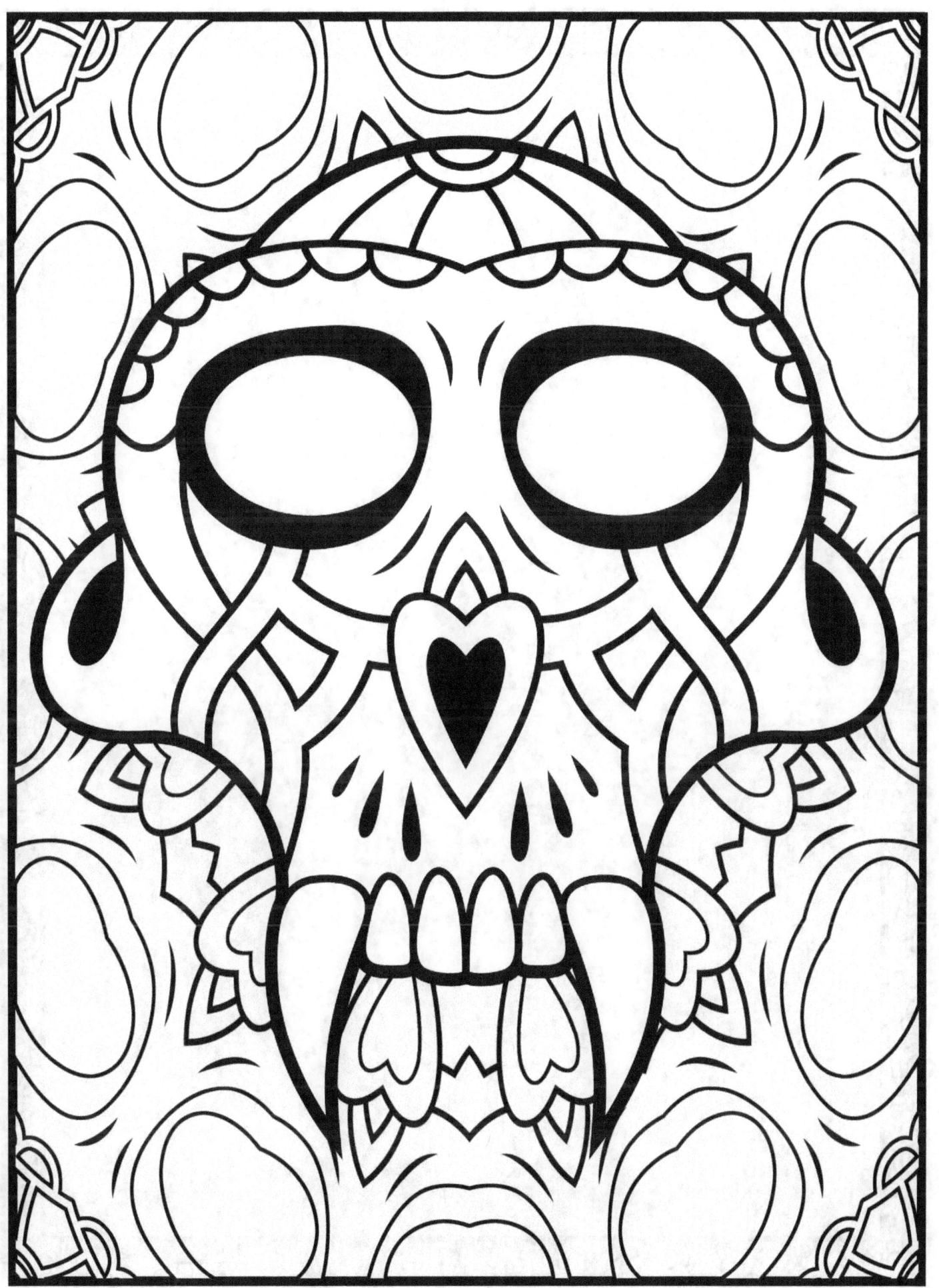

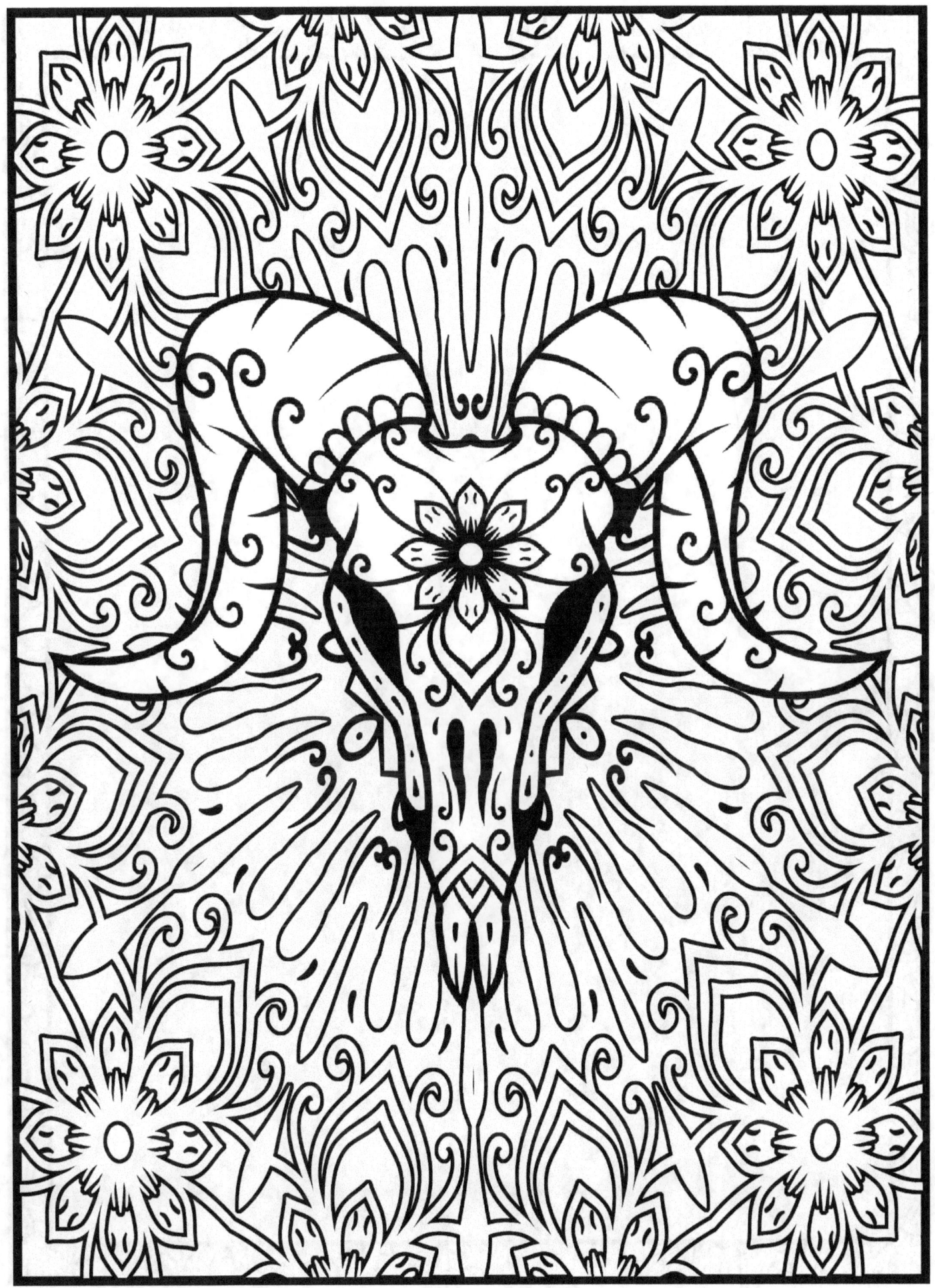

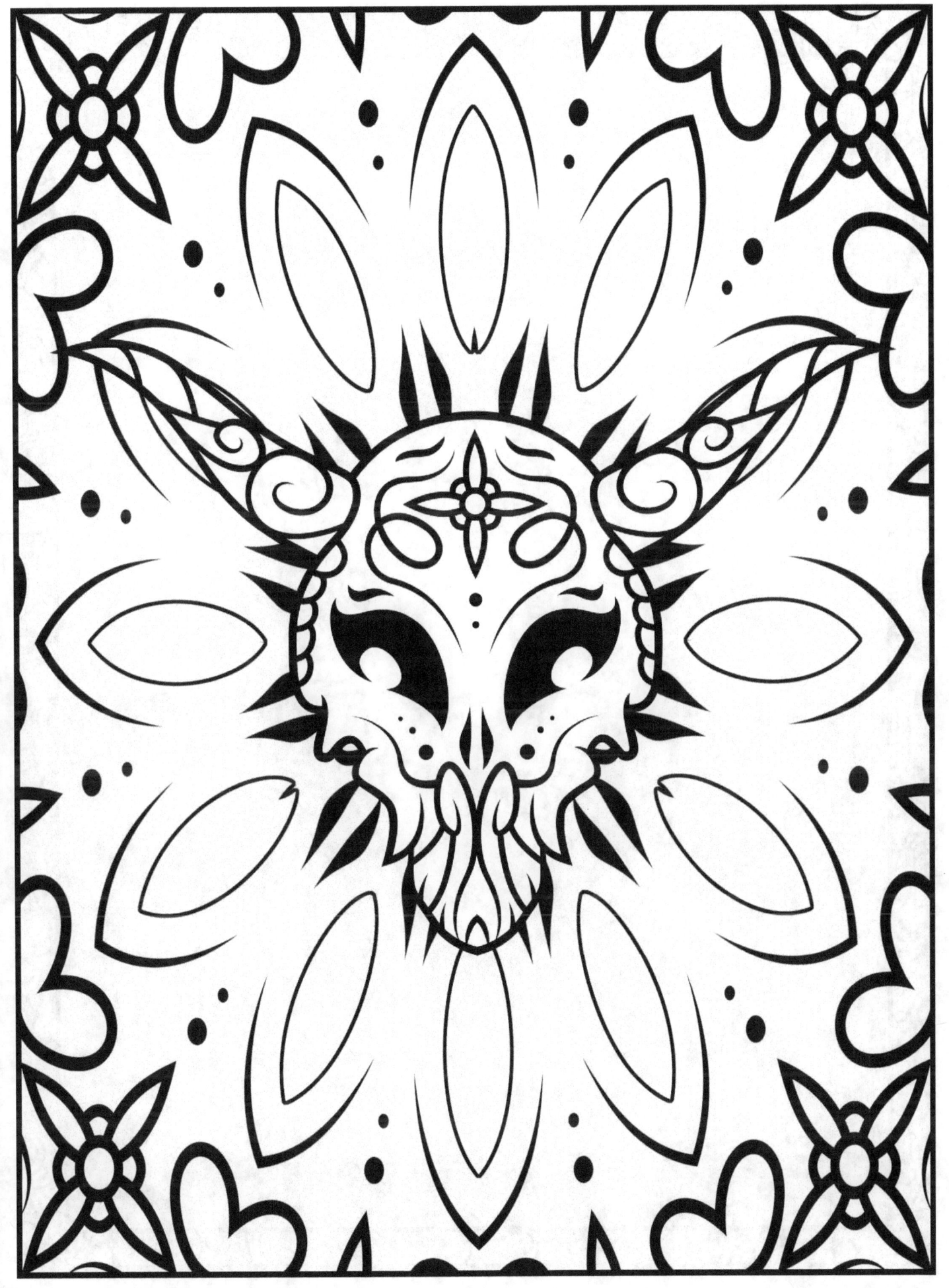

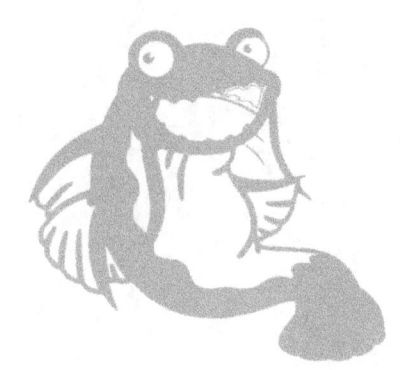

This Creepy Book was Created By

KatFishRiver

www.ingramcontent.com/pod-product-compliance
Lightning Source LLC
Chambersburg PA
CBHW082147230526
45467CB00043B/2375